THE
GREAT
REVERSAL

Evangelical Perspectives

John Warwick Montgomery, General Editor

HOW BLACK IS THE GOSPEL?
by Tom Skinner

THE UNEQUAL YOKE
by Richard V. Pierard

GOD, SEX AND YOU
by M. O. Vincent, M.D.

REVOLUTION AND THE CHRISTIAN FAITH
by Vernon C. Grounds

HOW DEPENDABLE IS THE BIBLE?
by Raymond F. Surburg

THE STONES AND THE SCRIPTURES
by Edwin M. Yamauchi

THE GREAT REVERSAL
by David O. Moberg

THE GREAT REVERSAL

Evangelism versus Social Concern

David O. Moberg

J.B. Lippincott Company
Philadelphia and New York / A HOLMAN BOOK

Acknowledgments

Grateful acknowledgment is made for permission to reprint with adaptations parts or all of the following articles by the author:

"Social Concern Versus Evangelism," *Gordon Review* [now published under the title *Christian Scholar's Review*], Vol. 10, No. 4 (Fall 1967), pp. 204-214 (portions in Chapters 1 and 8).

"Evangelical Christians in Contemporary Society: How to Reverse 'The Great Reversal,'" in *The Church in a Secular World: Papers Delivered at the Consultation on the Church in a Secular World, Oct. 11-13, 1967* (Wheaton, Ill.: National Association of Evangelicals, 1967), 34 pp., mimeographed (portions in Chapters 2 and 8).

"A Sociologist's View of Contemporary Christian Evangelism," *Mid-Stream,* Vol. 8, No. 4 (1970), pp. 17-31 (Chapter 4).

"Evangelism as a Motive for Social Welfare," Paper No. 2 in *The Role of the Christian through Church and State in Human Welfare* (Washington, D. C.: Baptist Joint Committee on Public Affairs, 1967), pp. 9-13 (Chapter 6).

U.S. Library of Congress Cataloging in Publication Data

Moberg, David O.
The great reversal.

"A Holman book."
Includes bibliographical references.
1. Evangelistic work.   2. Church and social problems.   I. Title.
BV3793.M56   261   72-2153
ISBN-O-87981-009-2

Contents

	Foreword	*8*
	Preface	*11*
1	*Evangelism versus Social Concern*	*13*
2	*The Great Reversal*	*28*
3	*Do Evangelicals Lack Social Concern?*	*46*
4	*The Sociological Analysis of Evangelism*	*67*
5	*Barriers to Effective Social Concern*	*86*
6	*Social Welfare and Evangelism*	*104*
7	*Social Sin*	*120*
8	*Reversing the Great Reversal*	*150*
	Suggestions for Further Reading	*183*
	Index	*186*

Foreword

A Perspective on "Evangelical Perspectives"

Across the centuries the Christian church has faced two perennial challenges: the maintenance of a pure testimony, and the application of revealed truth to the total life of man. Though these two tasks interlock (since application of the truth is impossible if the truth is lost, and truth without application stands self-condemned), theology has generally devoted itself now to the one, now to the other, and the cause of Christ has suffered from the imbalance. "These ought ye to have done, and not to leave the other undone" stands as a perpetual judgment over the church's history.

Today's theology and church life display such deleterious polarization in an especially gross manner. At the liberal end of the theological spectrum, efforts to become "relevant" have succeeded so well that the church has become indistinguishable from the ideological and societal evils she is supposed to combat. Among the fundamentalists, in contrast, God's revealed truth often serves as a wall to block the church off from the live issues and compelling challenges of a world in crisis. Relevance without truth, or truth without relevance: these dual schizophrenias go far in explaining why contemporary man finds it easy to ignore the Christian message.

Evangelical Perspectives is a series of books designed specifically to overcome these false dichotomies. Historic Christian theology—the Christianity of the Apostles' Creed, of the Protestant Reformation, and of the eighteenth-century Evangelical Revival—is taken with full seriousness, and is shown to be entirely compatible with the best of contemporary scholarship. Contributors to this series are united in rejecting the defensive posture which has so often created the impression that new knowledge poses a genuine threat to the Christian gospel. Axiomatic to the present series is the conviction that new discoveries serve but to confirm and deepen the faith once delivered to the saints.

At the same time, those participating in this project find little comfort in the reiteration of ancient truth for its own sake. Our age faces staggering challenges which can hardly be met by the repetition of formulas—certainly not by the negativistic codes of a fundamentalism which tilts against windmills that have long since fallen into decay. The race problem, social revolution, political change, new sexual freedom, the revival of the occult, the advent of the space age: these are areas of modern life that demand fresh analysis on the basis of the eternal verities set forth in the Word of One who is the same yesterday, today, and forever.

Out of the flux of the current theological situation nothing but flux appears to be emerging. What is needed is a firm foundation on which to build an all-embracing and genuinely relevant theological perspective for the emerging twenty-first century. The authors of the present volumes are endeavoring to offer just such a perspective— an *evangelical* perspective, a perspective arising from the biblical evangel—as the one path through the maze of contemporary life.

It is the hope of the editor that upon the solid Reformation base of a fully authoritative Scripture, the present series will offer its readers the Renaissance ideal of the Christian as *uomo universale.* Such an orientation could revolutionize theology in our time, and ground a new age of commitment and discovery comparable to that of the sixteenth century. As in that day, new worlds are opening up, and just as a religious viewpoint reflecting the dying medieval age was unable to meet the challenge then, so today's secular theologies are incapable of pointing the way now. The Christ of the Bible, through whom all without exception have been created and redeemed: He alone is Way, Truth, Life—and Perspective!

JOHN WARWICK MONTGOMERY
General Editor

Preface

I first heard Professor Timothy L. Smith's expression, "the Great Reversal," approximately a decade ago when he gave a lecture on revivalism and social reform at Bethel College and Seminary. It so neatly epitomized some of my own thoughts that it stuck in my mind, stimulating my thinking on the subject ever since. I hope it will do the same for all who read this book.

Some Christians may see the issue of relationships between evangelism and social concern—or, if you prefer, the personal and social dimensions of the Christian gospel—as an old and settled matter. The minister who is caught in the crossfire of conflict on the subject will certainly not agree with them.

Others may feel that discussions like this are merely "beating an old horse"; the church is dying, so why waste time trying to make it run again? Or to use another analogy, "You can't put new wine into old wineskins." But there is still a great deal of life left in many congregations, and some are adapting exceptionally, creatively, and redemptively to social crises and human needs.

In the preface to his excellent *Christian Manifesto,* Dr. Ernest T. Campbell, senior minister of the highly influential Riverside Church in New York City, has shared his opinion that the Christian church is in "danger of coming apart on the question of whether the gospel is personal or social." Each side suspects the Christian credentials of the other. The internal dispute threatens to complete the ruinous work that it has begun.

The unresolved polarities in current Christendom are like dynamite; they have the potential for either constructive or destructive explosions. I hope that this book will be constructive, contributing to reconciliation and peace between the warring factions.

My helpers have been legion. The special acts of consideration of my wife and children, given in the face of my own neglect of them while I was preparing for and writing the manuscript, deserve special recognition. The efficient typing of Mrs. Sharron Johns and the backup secretarial work of Mrs. Diane Willette have provided an obviously essential service. The book was stimulated considerably by problems raised during a year of work as a consultant to the National Liberty Foundation and the LaSalle Street Church of Chicago.

Dozens of scholars, students, colleagues, churchmen, and friends have assisted by means of conversations or correspondence. Among them are Clifford V. Anderson, Jack Balswick, Gordon Bear, Clifford Benzel, Ronald J. Cook, William W. Everett III, Ivan J. Fahs, Horace L. Fenton, Roland Foster, Roy G. Francis, Bernard Grunstra, James G. Harris, Pierre Hegy, Urban T. Holmes III, Donald N. Larson, Michael Leming, William H. Leslie, Gordon R. Lewis, Ruth McIntyre, Stephen Charles Mott, Elwin M. Mueller, William M. Pinson, Jr., Claude E. Stipe, Robert Voss, John Wells, and, of course, Russell T. Hitt and John Warwick Montgomery.

In every chapter I had to fight the impulse to develop an entire book-length treatise on the subject. I hope others will take up the challenge to develop and clarify these topics more thoroughly. Social science research, historical analysis, and theological study are needed on every aspect of the polarities and their reconciliation.

D. O. M.

Department of Sociology and Anthropology
Marquette University

Evangelism versus Social Concern

A salesclerk in a toy department was helping a mother and father purchase a gift for their child. As he demonstrated a three-dimensional puzzle, he used the educational appeal to their middle-class concern for the future status of their offspring: "This will prepare your child for growing up in the modern world—no matter how you put it together, it won't come out right!"[1]

Confronted with the tremendous number and the intricate complexity of social problems today, we are easily gripped by despair and tempted to feel that no matter what we do, it will be wrong. Like men in every age of history, we live in a world engulfed in social problems. As Jesus said, "The poor you always have with you . . . " (John 12:8).

Divisions in Christendom

The question of how to deal with poverty and the numerous other interrelated problems of our day has divided Christians into two camps. One of them builds a strong case for evangelism as the basic solution, while the other emphasizes direct social involvement. Each accuses the other of being untrue to the essential nature of Christianity. Each feels the other is hypocritical. Each charges the other with being a detriment to the Kingdom of God and the cause of Jesus Christ.

Sometimes during their battle skirmishes one gets the impression that they are like the junior boys in a Sunday school class in which the teacher was telling about the wonders of heaven and the contrasting horrors of hell. At the conclusion of the lesson she wanted an affirmation from the boys, a moment of decision to strengthen the impact of her teaching, so she asked all who wanted to go to heaven to raise their hands. Sure enough, all hands were raised—except that of one boy near the back of the room.

"Jimmy," she said to him, "don't you want to go to heaven?"

"No, ma'm, not if that's where those guys are going," was his astonishing reply.[2]

Divisions of opinion between "soul-winners" and "social gospelers" are sharp; sometimes they seem to produce cleavages as great as that which separated Jimmy from the other boys in his Sunday school class. It is tempting to think that they are outmoded relics from a generation that is past, but that is not yet true. The so-called "ecumenical wing" of Protestant Christianity tends to emphasize social involvement, while "fundamentalists" and "evangelicals" stress evangelism. These divergent orientations to social problems are among the most significant factors in the refusal of the latter groups to participate in the ecumenical movement.

An extraordinary amount of religious conflict came to a head during the 1920's. The Scopes trial centering on the evolution issue in 1925, heresy trials of clergymen and seminary professors, numerous polemic publications on doctrinal issues, and religious attacks upon higher education were among the events that captured national attention as the fundamentalist-modernist controversy reached its peak. Among the issues involved was the social theology of modernists who called for radical changes in society in contrast to the person-oriented and individualistic perspectives of Protestant conservatives. The social gospel of the liberals was no gospel at all to fundamentalists, who saw in the Bible only a gospel for saving individuals, not one for redeeming the social order.[3] Many splinter groups were formed as a result, and numerous independent fundamentalist and evangelical organizations were established for the fulfillment of specific missions. They have functioned as surrogate denominations for many individuals and church congregations.

The putative crisis in the American church in the seventies flows intelligibly from the altercations of the twenties and may be described as the alienation of the majority of churchmen from their duly constituted leadership in their attachment to causes represented by Billy Graham, Norman Vincent Peale, or the Civil Religion. . . . Though the exact issues have changed—primarily from ideas and institutions to human groups within society—the parallels between "only yesterday" and our new decade are captivating, and comparative reflection upon them is instructive.[4]

In a very real sense, then, the current tensions between those who emphasize personal versus social ministries in contemporary Christendom are a continuation of the fundamentalist-modernist controversies, even though details of the issues, terminology, and groups involved have changed. Today, as then, the struggle was at its most intense level within rather than between the respective denominational bodies. The cold war could burst into a religious battle as intense and destructive as the conflict of the 1910's and 1920's if no satisfactory resolution is reached for the central issues of evangelism and social concern. The Christian church "is confronted by no more menacing danger than the danger of coming apart on the question of whether the gospel is personal or social."[5]

The Great Reversal

Evangelism versus Social Concern

Expressing his expectations and hopes for the 1966 World Congress on Evangelism, Billy Graham wrote:

This cause of evangelism to which I have dedicated my life is now suffering from confusion. There is confusion about evangelism among both its enemies and its friends. The enemies of biblical evangelism—which demands a personal confrontation with the claims of Jesus Christ—are keeping the name but substituting another practice. The "new" evangelism says soul winning is passé. It wants to apply Christian principles to the social order. Its proponents want to make the prodigal son comfortable, happy and prosperous in the far country without leading him back to the Father.[6]

One of the reports following that congress included these comments:

. . . most of those who spoke during the early sessions were against an overemphasis of concern for social issues by today's churches. *Christianity Today's* news reports said the most common complaint among delegates was that the daily discussion groups opened up great issues without striving to arrive at any conclusion.

The relation of evangelism to social concern—to cite the major example—was a recurring theme, and many delegates felt there should have been more of an effort to crystallize thinking on it.

Some publications in America had predicted before the Congress that the meeting would turn into a debate between evangelism versus social action proponents. But such a debate never materialized, primarily because social action was not given much of a platform.[7]

The Methodist Consultation on Evangelism in Latin America, convened to re-evaluate the methods of evangelism in light of the great social changes occurring in Central and South America, pointed up the current relevance of this debate: "The two points of view on evangelism were never resolved: traditional evangelism which stresses preaching and personal evangelism versus greater emphasis on social action."[8]

At the Ninth Inter-Varsity Missionary Convention held at the University of Illinois in Urbana in December 1970, it became very apparent that the 12,000 students who attended were much less concerned about formal missions subjects than with the relationship between evangelism and social concern.[9] This may be due partly to the fact that within most American denominations today pressure groups are working on both sides of the controversy. Many are very loose interest groups, but some, like the Presbyterian Lay Committee, are highly organized. It was established to put greater emphasis upon the teaching of the Bible as the authoritative Word of God, to emphasize the need for evangelism, to encourage *individuals* to take their place of involvement in society but to urge official church bodies to refrain from issuing pronouncements or taking action on social, economic, and political affairs except under very restrictive conditions, and to disseminate information on significant issues confronting the United Presbyterian Church. Its monthly periodical, *The Presbyterian Layman,* indicates clearly that it views itself as a counterbalance to the social activism that has been apparent in recent years within the United Presbyterian Church.

Similarly, an executive of Lutheran Youth Encounter speaking to an adult class I visited in Calvary Baptist Church of St. Paul, Minnesota, on June 28, 1970, stated, "The polarization of social activists and those who want to get into the Word is very evident in the Lutheran Church." The Lutheran Men in America of Wisconsin (LMA) published their policy statement in an advertisement shortly before the 1971 convention of the Missouri

Synod met in Milwaukee. It included the following sentences:

LMA believe [*sic*] that the church should not become involved in secular politics, and believes that such involvement invites the entrance of politics into the church. We believe further that the modern social philosophy, as preached by some, is inappropriate in the church and offensive to some members . . . . [10]

This statement is consistent with the perspective of the Rev. Norman W. Berg, a Wisconsin Evangelical Lutheran Synod pastor who, as president of the Lutheran Free Conference, stated that the mission of the church is the salvation of souls, not the redemption of society; the latter "will be a natural by-product of the preaching of the gospel."[11]

Episcopalians similarly have been hit severely by the struggle of church involvement in social issues, the Foundation of Christian Theology even seeking to drive their church leadership out of office.[12] Concerned Presbyterians, Inc., are attempting to return the Presbyterian Church in the U.S. (Southern) to the basic purpose of leading unsaved souls to Christ in opposition to church leaders who favor a greater involvement in social issues. [13] Similar controversies are found among the United Methodists, Disciples of Christ, Roman Catholics, United Church of Christ, and virtually every major denomination. Even the Southern Baptist Convention is not exempt; Baptists United for Spiritual Revival were united by "a common concern over the tendencies of certain elements in the North Carolina Convention to lead us away from scriptural authority and basic evangelism towards theological liberalism and social activism,"[14] and the Evangelical Christian Education Foundation is a "conservative theological education projection" to combat liberalism in Southern Baptist seminaries.

The same concern is apparent in other nations. The 1969 meeting of the European Baptist Federation, which had 2,000 delegates in Vienna, was described in these words:

Tensions between those who emphasize the preaching of the gospel in the formal sense and those who heavily stress Christian social work were evident, as in every denomination.[15]

The problems are traced by the *Reader's Digest* to "the mood set by the World Council of Churches," for it allegedly supported programs to combat racism, giving aid to "liberation movements" which were engaged in guerrilla activities, avowedly communistic and with records of bloody terrorism, and it also aided American draft dodgers and deserters in Canada and Sweden. The leaders of the W.C.C. and denominations that have followed its example may merely have made "errors in judgment," or they may have lost faith in orderly change, being unsure of their mission and forgetful that Christianity's age-old weapons of reconciliation and love are needed to transform men and their societies.[16]

Unquestionably the problems of the various Christian bodies are interrelated; they may all be seen as part of the central question of whether evangelism or social concern is the more appropriate channel of Christian response to the complex problems of contemporary society.

Certain aspects of this controversy can be explored by means of what a sociologist might call "ideal types" of the evangelistic and social involvement approaches to social problems. These typological abstractions from the complex world of reality may seem like caricatures, for they deliberately accentuate contrasts of perspective and action between the two camps. They select certain key characteristics for the purpose of making the distinctions clear. In actual life, most persons and groups do not fall purely and completely into either category although most Christians tend to be inclined toward either one direction or the other.

Evangelism as the Solution for Social Problems

The evangelistic camp holds that the Christian has but one task—that of winning souls to Christ. The only important goal in life is to be a "fisher of men." In order to have stars in one's heavenly crown, he must win others to Christ.

Personal evangelism and mass revivalism are the summum bonum of the Christian life. All church-related programs and organizations should be oriented toward that end, and every worthwhile personal activity is designed to promote it. "He that winneth souls is wise" (Prov. 11:30) is a favorite Bible verse. Trophies for Christ are sought in somewhat the same way a big-game hunter in Africa stalks his exotic prey. Nonevangelistic activities like "church socials" and recreational events are permitted in church programming only as a bait to entice sinners into the net of the Kingdom of Jesus Christ. Revivalism is emphasized and, as a chapel speaker in Bethel College, St. Paul, Minnesota, once stated it, "The revival meeting is like a pressure cooker—to increase the heat, one simply increases the pressure."

Since soul-winning is the chief goal, little direct attention is given to social problems except to relate them to that main objective. In fact, some evangelistic Christians are delighted to observe that conditions in the world are far from perfect. They believe that problems people face will drive them to Jesus Christ, Who is *the* answer to all personal and social ills. If men will only put their trust in

Him, He will make all things work together for good. Conversion will either solve their problems or give them strength and grace to bear them.

Other evangelistic Christians are delighted at the mess the world is in because they know that "evil men and seducers shall wax worse and worse, deceiving, and being deceived" (II Tim. 3:13). Their eschatological interpretation of history holds that the destiny of human society is one of progressive degeneration, deterioration, and devolution until the establishment of Christ's millennial Kingdom. The worse things get, the closer His coming must be, so they rejoice.

A few fundamentalists seem also to have an implicit idea that there is a specific quota of souls to be won for the heavenly Kingdom; when the last soul is won, Christ will return for His own; soul-winning therefore is "hastening the coming" of the Lord. He will rescue the world from its mess by establishing the perfect society; therefore, soul-winning is the chief means of solving social problems.

Interestingly, some evangelistic Christians who focus upon soul-winning as the solution to social problems also become directly involved in certain political issues. They attempt to establish prohibition of the sale and use of alcoholic beverages through the exercise of local option; they try to censor newsstands or local library holdings in order to control the problem of obscenity; or they campaign for a favorite candidate to the office of county sheriff so that they will be allowed to hold religious services in the jail. Their efforts to cope with selected social problems generally reflect moral indignation and are oriented toward those that directly and obviously involve "personal sins." Their assumption is that controlling personal deviations is a means for extending the opportunity of people to hear the gospel and thus a tool in soul-winning.

Closer to the mainstream of the American religious population are those evangelistic Christians who look at social problems from a slightly different perspective. They hold that conversion to Jesus Christ changes lives in a wholesome manner. The decision for Christ will make a dishonest man become honest; a criminal, law-abiding; a sexual pervert, upright; an improvident man, provident; a mentally ill person, well; a corrupt politician, clean; a lazy worker, ambitious; a rapacious businessman, kind; a greedy self-seeker, generous; a self-centered introvert, other-oriented. When people are converted, they will generously support private welfare plans that will so adequately meet the needs of the downtrodden that no government welfare will be needed. Since they believe that all social problems are at root merely personal problems, these evangelistic Christians think that solving personal problems through converting souls to Jesus Christ will resolve all the problems of the world. Soul-winning is thus seen as the very highest form of social concern.

I need not describe this position further. It is one all evangelicals know and sympathize with deeply, much as they may criticize certain details of thought and action related to it.

Social Involvement in Human Problems

The other "ideal or pure type" of Christian position in relationship to human problems teaches that the first is in error on several counts. It holds that evangelistic Christians fail to recognize that the expression, "Christ is the answer," is often used as an excuse for inaction and leaves the solution of problems up to His direct intervention; Christians as citizens and as children of God should step instead into the political and social arena to cope with problems of injustice and suffering. Washing one's hands of God-given social responsibility violates the stewardship trust that dates back to the Garden of Eden. To be true to God's will, the Christian must stretch out in love to bind up the bleeding wounds of humanity and to prevent future suffering.

Labeling as "hypocrites" those who emphasize a personal gospel as the sole solution to man's needs, socially involved Christians view deeds of kindness as ends in themselves rather than as "bait" to entice others to Christ or the church. Doing good is for them the highest form of preaching, for they see it as conveying the message of God's love to all mankind by deeds and example.

One of their chief emphases is the fact that evil is deeply entrenched in man's social systems. The highly moral man who lives in a society permeated with subtle social evils may promulgate those evils even through his personally "moral" behavior.[17] For instance, most Germans under the Nazis were kind, honorable, loving, family men obedient to the scriptural injunction to "be subject to the governing authorities" (Rom. 13:1). Yet many of them served methodically and carefully in clerical, construction, transportation, and other tasks related to the genocide of the Jews and the incarceration of people from conquered nations, thus becoming accomplices in the moral evils of their leaders even when they appeared outwardly and felt inwardly that they were doing no ill to anyone.

These Christians recognize that focusing on personal morals alone does not solve social problems. Only as the evils of society and its basic institutions are rooted out can true morality be established. Therefore they insist that the battle against sin must be waged against inequities and injustices in the social order that twist the personal lives of individuals and do violence to their high status as creatures made in the image of God.

Most of the basic doctrines of this perspective came to be known as the Social Gospel early in this century. Walter Rauschenbusch, one of its most prominent leaders, put it in these words:

As long as a man sees in our present society only a few inevitable abuses and recognizes no sin and evil deep-seated in the very constitution of the present order, he is still in a state of moral blindness and without conviction of sin. Those who believe in a better social order are often told that they do not know the sinfulness of the human heart. They could justly retort the charge on the men of the evangelical school. When the latter deal with public wrongs, they often exhibit a curious unfamiliarity with the forms which sin assumes there, and sometimes reverently bow before one of the devil's spider-webs, praising it as one of the mighty works of God. Regeneration includes that a man must pass under the domination of the spirit of Christ, so that he will judge of life as Christ would judge of it. That means a revaluation of social values. Things that are now "exalted among men" must become "an abomination" to him because they are built on wrong and misery. Unless a man finds his judgment at least on some fundamental questions in opposition to the current ideas of the age, he is still a child of this world and has not "tasted the powers of the coming age."

. . . No man can help the people until he is himself free from the spell which the present order has cast over our moral judgment. . . . every social institution weaves a protecting integument of glossy idealization about itself like a colony of tent-caterpillars in an apple tree. For instance, wherever militarism rules, war is idealized by monuments and paintings, poetry and song.[18]

Rauschenbusch referred also to the fictions of capitalism which 'nold, for instance, that the poor are poor through their own fault, to the "complacent self-deception of those who profit by present conditions and are loath to believe that their life is working harm," and to "the warping influence of self-interest," as when tiny children were driven to the looms with whips in early nineteenth-century England while mill owners insisted that English industry would be ruined by proposed reform laws.[19]

Evaluation of the Two Approaches

It is far easier, alas, to see institutionalized inconsistencies from a distance in time and place than it is to see them in our own households or our own front and back yards. According to the socially involved, the solution to this problem of social sin is to reform the social order; but according to the evangelistic group it is to win souls to Christ so that new moral values will prevail in person-to-person relationships. And each accuses the other of hypocrisy.

As an evangelical, I am tempted to choose the better side! But I sense the inadequacies of both positions and suggest that neither is fully scriptural. The theme of this book is that there is a more excellent alternative. As in the case of numerous other controversies that have divided Christians, Scripture passages to support either ideal-type position may be found easily. Consequently, the rejection of either the evangelistic or the social-involvement perspective in favor of the other does violence to some of the clear teachings of the Bible. To succumb to either extreme to the exclusion of the other is to sin against God and man. The Christian who tries to live according to the full counsel of God will not get caught on the horns of this dilemma.

There was a time when evangelicals had a balanced

position that gave proper attention to both evangelism and social concern, but a great reversal early in this century led to a lopsided emphasis upon evangelism and omission of most aspects of social involvement (see Chapter 2). Since that time their shortcomings in regard to the fulfillment of Christian social responsibility have been very apparent (see Chapter 3). Sociological analysis of evangelism can help to shed light on this complex subject (see Chapter 4). Cultural and religious impediments stand in the way of its solution (see Chapter 5), but a considerable body of evidence supports the conclusion that evangelism can be a motive for social welfare (see Chapter 6) and can play an important role in social action to change society and deal with social sin (see Chapter 7). These facts are helping to reverse the Great Reversal, bringing new winds of the Spirit into contemporary evangelicalism and offering the potential of restoring it to its rightful place of leadership in regard to the social implications of the Christian faith (see Chapter 8).

Notes

[1] Adapted from a cartoon described by Kenneth L. Maxwell, *New on the UN Skyline* (New York: National Council of Churches, 1962), p. 3.

[2] Adapted from E. Francis Bowditch, "The Search for Values in Education," in Arthur E. Traxler, ed., *Long-Range Planning for Education* (Washington, D. C.: American Council on Education, 1958), pp. 28-29.

[3] David O. Moberg, *The Church as a Social Institution* (Englewood Cliffs, N. J.: Prentice-Hall, 1962), pp. 280-299.

[4] Samuel S. Hill, Jr., in book review of Willard B. Gatewood, Jr., ed., *Controversy in the Twenties: Fundamentalism, Modernism, and Evolution* (Nashville: Vanderbilt University Press, 1969), *Journal for the Scientific Study of Religion*, Vol. IX, No. 2 (Summer 1970), pp. 162, 163.

[5] Ernest T. Campbell, *Christian Manifesto* (New York: Harper & Row, 1970), p. ix.

[6]Billy Graham, "What We Expect at the Berlin Congress," *World Vision Magazine,* Vol. X, No. 9 (October 1966), p. 4.

[7]"Evangelicals Demonstrate Unity on Urgency of World Evangelism," *Home Missions* (Southern Baptist Convention), Vol. XXXVIII, No. 1 (January 1967), p. 21.

[8]Mrs. Edward Barber, Methodist missionary, as quoted in "Consultation on Evangelism Stresses Flexibility in Methods," *World Vision Magazine,* Vol. X, No. 9 (October 1966), p. 17.

[9]"Urbana 70 Message," *His Magazine,* Vol. XXXI, No. 6 (March 1971), pp. 1-11; Paul Fromer, "Acid Test," *ibid.,* p. 16.

[10]*Milwaukee Journal,* June 19, 1971, Pt. 1, p. 4.

[11]"Church's Role Spiritual, Not Social, Free Conference Told," *The Lutheran Layman,* Vol. XXXVII, No. 8 (August 1966), p. 6.

[12]"Episcopalians Face Challenge on Contributions to Blacks, Poor," *Milwaukee Journal,* October 10, 1970, Pt. 1, p. 4.

[13]"Split Among Presbyterians Seen," *Milwaukee Journal,* December 14, 1968, p. 4; "Presbyterians: Concern v. Concerned," *Time,* Vol. XC, No. 15 (October 13, 1967), p. 50.

[14]"North Carolina Baptists Organize," *Newsletter,* The Evangelical Christian Education Foundation, December 1970, p. 2.

[15]Lawrence C. Bowser, "Baptists of Europe Hear a Call to Abandon Longstanding Traditions," *Crusader,* Vol. XXIV, No. 11 (November 1969), p. 15.

[16]Clarence W. Hall, "Must Our Churches Finance Revolution?" *Reader's Digest,* Vol. L (October 1971), pp. 95-100. Numerous responses to this critique criticize its errors of fact and interpretation.

[17]Cf. Reinhold Niebuhr, *Moral Man and Immoral Society* (New York: Charles Scribner's Sons, 1932).

[18]Walter Rauschenbusch, *Christianity and the Social Crisis* (New York: Macmillan, 1907), pp. 349-350.

[19]*Ibid.,* pp. 350-351.

Social history in England and the United States clearly reveals that evangelical Christianity played a major role in both social reconstruction and social welfare. Earle E. Cairns, for instance, has shown the profound impact evangelical Christians had upon the abolition of slavery, prison reform, humane treatment of the mentally ill, and improved working conditions for industrial laborers.[1] They were highly instrumental in developing many concrete principles and forms of social work which prevail today.[2]

Numerous welfare societies were established by evangelicals to alleviate the effects of social evils.[3] Some of these arose out of a compassion awakened by nineteenth-century revivalists. Their position was one of "liberalism" in regard to social issues, for they recognized the social context, the social implications, the social causes, and the social effects of personal sin. The revivalism of a century ago was clearly related to the fulfillment of Christian social responsibility.[4] Charles G. Finney's impact upon central New York in the mid-1820's was so great that the area long remained a fruitful source of benevolent sympathies and funds, to mention but one example.[5]

When evangelicals entered the slums as soul-winners, they learned first hand the conditions under which people lived and quickly added social welfare programs. Such great evangelical leaders as F. B. Meyer, John H. Jowett,

Charles H. Spurgeon, and T. deWitt Talmadge thus
played a significant part in the establishment of gospel
missions, employment bureaus, orphanages, and other
agencies to meet the needs of the poor. They recognized
that more tangible help was needed by converts than a
mere blessing, "Go and sin no more." They founded the
Florence Crittenton Homes, the Salvation Army, industrial institutes, schools for immigrants, and other associations, programs, and services for the lower classes and
other people caught in the grip of unfortunate circumstances. They worked for the right of labor to strike for
higher wages, laws to control child labor, and legislation
to prevent the exploitation of women. They saw the poor
as victims of circumstances who were not to be blamed
for their plight, and they fought for the worth of fallen
women. Because they were true friends of the poor and
actively helped to meet their material and physical needs,
their evangelistic efforts among them were effective. They
brought the gospel of salvation, but they also played a
part in bringing about major societal reforms of the
nineteenth and early twentieth centuries. Their large
numbers and fervent commitment made them the most
important force in the nation's first war on poverty.[6]

The Salvation Army and other new evangelical denominations were oriented primarily toward the underprivileged. The Church of the Nazarene, for example, was
established with the chief aim of preaching holiness to
the poor. Its first stationery bore the verse, "Inasmuch as
ye have done it unto one of the least of these my brethren,
ye have done it unto me." Not only through evangelistic
outreach in both the church and door-to-door visitation,
but also through city missions, distribution of food,
shelter and clothing, direct care for the poor, comfort to
the dying, visiting the sick and imprisoned, sustaining

rest homes for unwed mothers, and other ministries to the
needy, they attempted to plant "centers of holy fire"
which would help to stem the tide of social evil.[7]

First-hand knowledge of poverty was amalgamated
with Christian compassion to deliver many of our evangelical forebears from the devastating interpretation that
sees misfortune as solely a product of personal failure and
sin.

The reality of "structural poverty" arising out of the
very nature of institutional organization in an industrial
society did not dawn as early upon others, however. The
latter had a strong tendency to see Christian social
responsibility only in terms of *welfare* to alleviate problems that had already arisen, not in terms of *social action*
to get at the causal roots of the problems in an effort to
prevent them from claiming more victims. An individualistic and moralistic orientation made them see the sources
in terms of personal good and evil and blinded them to
social causes that could not be attributed directly to
individuals. Yet their attempts to speak up for the underprivileged and to protect the interests of the laboring
classes marked many of them as champions of the poor.

The Great Reversal

From approximately 1910 until the 1930's, however, a
major shift in the position of evangelicals on social issues
occurred, a shift which historian Timothy L. Smith has
termed "the Great Reversal" in some of his lectures. For
example, Nazarene leaders who had been strongly sympathetic to the labor movement became antipathetic toward
it after World War I. Their social welfare work suffered
from steadily increasing neglect. When pronouncements
were made on social issues, they were buried in committee reports dealing with church members' standards of

personal behavior. Deaconesses declined in numbers and influence, and prohibitionism was reinterpreted in terms of personal salvation rather than social regeneration.[8]

Other evangelical groups similarly abandoned liberal political and economic perspectives. The intense interest in social service on the part of early Christian and Missionary Alliance members was soon subtly opposed by its founder, possibly because this competed with institutional goals of the new fellowship.[9]

A parallel inversion occurred in the Episcopal Church. Between 1880 and 1910 a large number of parish houses were constructed in response to the physical, recreational, educational, and other social needs of immigrants and laborers. Typically five or six stories high, they included classrooms, an assembly hall, a kitchen, parlors, a gymnasium, and even billiard rooms. They were designed to meet the needs of others and were only secondarily for their own members. But after World War I their uses shifted to more self-centered purposes for the parishioners.[10]

The isolationism that followed World War I, the growing pessimism of erstwhile believers in the inevitable progress of man, and numerous other unusual features of American society at that time may have played a part in the complex pattern of developments, but our analysis and examples will reveal that other factors seem to be more logical explanations of the Great Reversal.

Illustrations of the Great Reversal

Evangelist A. C. Dixon edited *The Fundamentals,* a twelve-volume series beginning in 1909, which became the rallying point of the fundamentalist movement. He also was noted for his attack upon the Social Gospel movement. During a Boston pastorate that began in 1901, his church administered an endowment of a million dollars, the interest from which was to be used for social service in the parish. At first

> ... it seemed to him like common sense that if they fed the hungry, paid their rent, and gave them a good doctor and medicine, it would be good preparation for preaching the gospel to them. But when, at the end of three years, Dixon realized that soul-winning did not follow body healing, he decided to "dispense with the whole business and get back to first principles." ... He learned that it "is immensely easier to reach a man's body through his soul, than his soul through his body."[11]

As a result of this experience, Dixon attacked the "false evangelism, which hoped to save society in bulk by means of humanitarian work," insisting that society could be saved only through true evangelism, the divine act of making individuals truly Christian.[12]

Similar perspectives had emerged somewhat earlier in the thinking of Dwight L. Moody. In an era of strong belief in the idea of progress, postmillennialists in the Social Gospel movement taught that the golden age of society was right around the corner, about to usher in the personal return of Christ. Moody considered this rank heresy. To him the world was a wrecked vessel; "God had commissioned Christians to use their lifeboats to rescue every man they could."[13] The world would get worse and worse until the Second Coming of Christ to establish His spiritual reign on earth for a thousand years. Christians therefore should set their affections in a heavenly direction; home, food, clothes, health, and financial security would follow for those who would first seek the Kingdom of God and His righteousness. Poverty would be overcome when diligence would replace indolence.[14]

Moody knew little about the scholarly and technical aspects of alcoholism, labor relations, and similar subjects, but he knew much about the misery of the masses that resulted from drunkenness, jobless families, and the poverty, disease, and filth of the slums. He knew that every man was a sinner in need of salvation, and he believed that

Before any of the ills of his personal, family, or community life could be looked to, he had to commit himself to the Nazarene as Lord and Saviour. If Christ was no panacea, at least He was the starting point, from which the convert could begin to leaven society.[15]

In addition to theological reasons for aloofness from direct social action, Moody received much of his financial support from wealthy businessmen and became exposed much more to their viewpoints on such issues as strikes and the Haymarket Riot than he was to those of poor laborers.[16] Undoubtedly this colored his perspectives and lent support to his opinion that attempts at social reform were a waste of time and diverted energy from the eternally beneficial work of soul-winning.

Billy Sunday in the early twentieth century followed Moody's example in believing that it was impossible to reform people *en masse,* that social reform begins with the individual. The purpose of Christianity to him was to save souls, not society; he saw the Social Gospel as nothing more nor less than socialism. Sunday added the strong assumption that the American Way of Life was a goal to be sought by all Christians, but even while attacking the amoral captains of industry and the heavy concentration of wealth in the United States, he strongly supported the laissez-faire doctrine of free enterprise. He engaged in zealous crusading against contemporary evils, chiefly on the level of personal vices. Except for his fervent efforts on behalf of Prohibition, he did not favor legislative reforms to alleviate suffering in the slums. The way to help the poor was not to educate them or to provide social services but to convert them to Jesus Christ. Those who rejected the gospel were hardened sinners who deserved whatever punishment or suffering came to them.[17]

Some Causes of the Great Reversal

These examples illustrate the fact that, as the fundamentalist-modernist controversies developed during the early part of this century, carrying out Christian social responsibility through attempts to influence legislation and basic social structures became identified with the Social Gospel movement, which had shifted gradually away from the evangelical tradition that had been evident in some of its early leaders. As the Social Gospel increased its interest in "secular" perspectives and issues and decreased its attention to directly biblical concerns and the spiritual needs of individual persons, it became linked with theological liberalism. It gave growing attention to social evils, while fundamentalists concentrated upon personal sin and individualistic approaches to social problems. It overemphasized man's horizontal relationships (man-to-man), while conservatives accentuated the vertical (man-to-God) and forgot the horizontal.[18] Each group read different parts of the Bible; when it stumbled into the other's domain, it provided a different interpretative schema. The sharp polarization that developed during the conflict made it politically impossible to remain both an evangelical and a social gospeler, and emotional involvements prevented Christians from recognizing the fallacies of being impaled upon the horns of a false dilemma. Christians became either evangelistic or socially involved, not both.

The enormity and complexity of the problems of urbanization and industrialization overwhelmed the efforts of religious philanthropists and led many of them to shake their heads in despair, concluding that they could do little about human wretchedness except to pray and try to evangelize their neighbors. The Bible does not specifically address itself to most modern problems, so those trying to "live by the Book" found nothing literal to guide them into social concern.[19]

Many Protestants became identified with the prosperous, moved their residences and churches away from the inner city with its "new immigrants" from southern and eastern Europe or the American South, and thus remained blind to many of the evils of their society.[20] The general social pessimism during and since World War I, the dispensational theology of many fundamentalists, and the fear of immigrants, Catholics, and Jews who were concentrated in large cities also contributed to the Great Reversal.[21]

Carl F. H. Henry believes that the dearth of evangelical social concern is partly due (1) to neglect of the good news of salvation for sinners by social gospelers, for that imposed upon conservatives the staggering burden of biblical evangelism and missions throughout the world, (2) to the decimation of evangelical capability by liberal control of such ecclesiastical resources as the denominations and schools, and most of all (3) to the reaction against Protestant liberals' attempts to achieve the Kingdom of God on earth through political and economic changes, excluding the supernatural redemptive facets of Christian faith.[22]

This suggests that a part of the reason for the Great Reversal was the concentration by evangelicals upon other legitimate issues. Attempting to hold firm to the faith that had been delivered once and for all, they confused it with cultural values that had been relevant on the nineteenth-century frontier but had become increasingly irrelevant in twentieth-century cities. Just as they disregarded biblical teaching on the stewardship of creation by floating "down the stream of commonly accepted values and by concentrating on *other*—often legitimate—theological and ethical problems,"[23] so they developed blind spots to current social evils by focusing their attack upon the kinds of individualistic evils that were especially prominent in wide-open frontier towns.[24]

Tensions between the prophetic and the priestly orientations to Christian ministries may have played a part. The priestly-pastoral concerns for relating individuals to God and helping them in the hour of special need was retained as a focus in evangelicalism, but the prophetic call to repent collectively as a people and reform society was rejected, partly because the social gospelers were moving heavily in that direction. Failure to see the close, complementary relationships between the two approaches, partly because Jesus' own example seems on the surface to focus exclusively upon healing and helping individual persons, probably accentuated the avoidance of social reform, as did the failure to see how necessary justice is to love.

John Warwick Montgomery has indicated that the root cause of "the terrible anomaly of socially retarded evangelical Christianity having the only absolute Word and eternal motivation capable of binding up a fallen world" is evangelicals' lack of consistency with their profession that they accept *all* of the Scripture, not, like liberals, accepting only what they like.

But why don't we follow our own advice? The liberals use the visible scissors and paste of destructive biblical criticism while we employ the invisible scissors and paste of selective hermeneutics: we preach only those texts that do not make us socially uncomfortable.[25]

As a result, nineteenth-century shibboleths are elevated to revelatory status; the mold of the old fundamentalist-modernist controversy is allowed to condition the basic response to social problems; traditions like laissez-faire individualism are baptized and used to emasculate and encapsulate "the whole counsel of God."[26] Even while claiming not to be conformed to this world, evangelicals are subtly squeezed into its mold (Rom. 12:1-2). Such sinful conformity is especially great in regard to Christian social responsibility.

Numerous other factors—all of which are insufficiently researched—undoubtedly played a part in the Great Reversal that made evangelicals become aloof from active social involvement early in this century. Among these are the diversion of fervor into anti-evolutionary conflicts and battles with theological liberals, the feeling that Prohibition would solve all social ills, the premillennialist doctrine that all social conditions would inevitably and irreversibly grow increasingly worse until the Second Coming of Jesus Christ, the belief that only the establishment of the millennial Kingdom of Christ could cure social problems, the false doctrine that New Testament admonitions to Christian love apply to the material welfare of only brethren in Christ, the dichotomic fallacy that the Christian message must be either personal or social, either spiritual or social, and either this-worldly or other-worldly and cannot be both, "the gospel of individual piety" which has led many selfishly to try to escape from the world and live lazily in separation from it while waiting for Christ's coming instead of working in it until His return, and similar indirect consequences of fundamentalist commitments.[27] These made theological conservatives shun social involvement as "the poison of social gospelers,"[28] a tendency that is still common in the

1970's. Much of the polemic from both sides of the contest between evangelism and social action represents negative reactions against real or alleged errors, abuses, and deficiencies of the past.

Rescue missions and church-sponsored welfare institutions to serve the aged and homeless children were continued after the Great Reversal, to be sure, and there were occasional crusades related to "blue laws," local political corruption, and personal vices, but on the whole society was denounced as evil and as either totally unredeemable or else subject to reconstruction only by the conversion of individuals.

Conservatism and Right-Wing Extremism

As a result of the Great Reversal, conservatism in theology often is equated today with conservatism in economic, political, and social affairs. One who is labeled as a "conservative evangelical" is rather automatically assumed also to be in or very near to the position of political right-wing extremists. The efforts by some of our evangelical brethren to make their socially conservative position known and their preachments implying that the only Christian position on key issues is one that coincides with the vested interests of the wealthy help to alienate conscientious youth, the laboring classes, racial minorities, and poor people from them. Without realizing its implications, they have adopted many tenets of the Social Darwinists.[29]

The linkage of fundamentalism with the extreme right in politics is not a result of an opportunism seeking to receive the benefits of pleasing wealthy patrons. It represents a striving for self-consistency and reflects the tendency of all men to link what they hate religiously with what they hate politically. Anti-communism and anti-modernism have been united in their minds. Richard Hofstadter suggests they may have "generically preju-diced minds" and that their "secularized fundamental-ism"

has yielded a type of pseudo-political mentality whose way of thought is best understood against the historical backgrounds of the revivalist preacher and the camp meeting. The fundamental-ist mind has had the bitter experience of being routed in the field of morals and censorship, on evolution and Prohibition, and it finds itself increasingly submerged in a world in which the great and respectable media of mass communication violate its sensibilities and otherwise ignore it. In a modern, experi-mental, and "sophisticated" society, it has been elbowed aside and made a figure of fun. . . . [30]

But "secularized fundamentalism" found in politics a new force and a new punitive capacity as it allied itself with other "one-hundred percenters" who will tolerate no ambiguities, compromises, equivocations, reservations, or criticisms.[31] The unfortunate tendency of too many evangelical laymen to believe that if a man's "theology" sounds correct he must also be correct in his political and socioeconomic views helps to win contributing sup-porters of that movement. Meanwhile a similar tendency of nonevangelical Christians to lump together everybody who is theologically to their right brings the onus of the politically right-wing fundamentalists upon all evangeli-calism.

The folly of unequally yoking political conservatism with evangelical Christianity has been demonstrated ef-fectively by Richard V. Pierard.[32] Senator Mark Hatfield also has gone on record as to how his conservative Protestant theology impelled him to become one of the leading liberals in his political party.[33]

The Great Reversal

Current Evangelical Social Response

When new social issues arise in society or when there is a new awareness of the problematic nature of old conditions, theologians of neo-orthodox, liberal, neo-liberal, and other nonevangelical positions discuss them. Groups within the National Council of the Churches of Christ in the U.S.A. then speak up, presenting what they believe to be a Christian position on the issue. Typically, that position is then attacked by evangelicals with the help of clichés, appeals to tradition, and proof texts that fit their preconceived conclusions. Eventually major groups in society, if not government itself, take positions and initiate actions that are to a considerable extent in line with the N.C.C.'s ethical recommendations or resolutions. Social pressures upon evangelicals then mount; they must take a stand, so they begin careful study of the issue. Eventually they arrive at the same practical conclusions as most other Christians who took a stand ten to thirty or more years earlier, even if it is on the basis of slightly different theological assumptions, rationale, or theoretical grounds.[34]

If this is an accurate summary of the typical pattern of evangelical action, it is to our disgrace. Instead of being a generation behind the times, we who are "people of the Book" ought to be in the prophetic forefront of our society. If we truly are filled with the compassionate love of Christ, we ought to be the first to seek means of alleviating the suffering of the masses as well as of the few persons among them whom we happen to discover. If we honestly are attempting to seek first the Kingdom of God, we ought to be the last to adopt sociopolitical positions which are selfishly oriented toward heaping up treasures on earth. If we truly are followers of the Christ

Who came to proclaim good tidings to the poor (Luke 4:18) and if we heed the scriptural admonition to "remember the poor," we ought to lift our voices on behalf of them who otherwise have few advocates or none in public life.

In fact, however, it often seems as if we evangelicals are just the opposite from what we ought to be. We wait until there is general consensus in society before we speak on controversial issues in a pattern of "me-too-ism" that makes us almost like contemporary ancestors of the present generation. We focus upon personal vices and individual problems, failing to see that the great sweeping social problems of our time also are personal problems for all their victims. We defend "the rights of property" when they clash with the physical, psychological, or intellectual welfare of underprivileged people. We hail the class-related positions of the rich with rationalizing Scripture passages and salve our consciences for neglecting the poor by giving out a few Thanksgiving baskets and making token contributions to a gospel mission. If our neighborhood begins to deteriorate and poor whites or Negroes begin to invade it, we move our homes and churches to the suburbs so that we can avoid direct confrontation with "those incompatible people whom it is impossible to reach with the gospel." When told that there is poverty and suffering in our own community, we point to television antennae on the homes of the poor and say it is their own fault if they buy TVs instead of bread. With a host of additional rationalizations, including abused social statistics and appeals to what *we* know *they* really want and we understand better than they "what is best for them," we selfishly defend ourselves for not acting on behalf of the misfortunate people in society——and thus we betray our Lord.

A major source of the rigid equation of sociopolitical conservatism with evangelicalism is conformity with the world. We have equated Americanism with Christianity to such an extent that we are tempted to believe that people in other cultures must adopt American institutional patterns when they are converted. We are led through natural psychological processes to an unconscious belief that the essence of our American Way of Life is basically, if not entirely, Christian.

Not only are evangelicals conformed to society, but a large proportion of them also are strongly inclined to do all within their power to keep society conformed to its present shape. The resulting implication is that there is no room for improvement, hence that society is either hopelessly lost or else that it already is God's best for man. If we truly believed the present social order to be evil, would we not do whatever is in our power to overcome that evil? To hold that no change is better than any change is to imply that the present state of affairs is nearer to a Christ-honoring position than any other possible alternative could be. To insist that a return to conditions of the nineteeth century should be our goal is to set up that century as something akin to the millennium.

A century ago evangelicals were in the forefront of social concern, but now we have become so identified with "the successful," in terms of this world's ideologies, that we put brakes on nearly every proposal for dealing with social problems in a manner consistent with the realities of our complex urban-industrial world. Instead of helping to alleviate the ills of the poor and underprivileged, we react against those who try to do so. Some even boast, as a prominent evangelical leader did in a major address I heard in September 1967, "With all the clamor about the poor and minorities in our society, it's time someone speaks up in defense of White Anglo-Saxon Protestant Puritans. I'm for the upper dog."

Is it any wonder that sensitive youth turn against the hypocrisies of such leaders? Evangelicals who defend the wealthy and powerful who are "grinding the face of the poor" (Isa. 3:15) in a selfish drive for earthly gain are in danger of hearing the judgment curse of the Lord (Matt. 25: 41-46) as well as the curses of earthly protest movements.

Notes

[1]Earle E. Cairns, *Saints and Society* (Chicago: Moody Press, 1960). See also Bertram Wyatt-Brown, *Lewis Tappan and the Evangelical War against Slavery* (Cleveland: Press of Case Western Reserve University, 1969).

[2]Kathleen Heasman, *Evangelicals in Action: An Appraisal of Their Social Work in the Victorian Era* (London: Geoffrey Bles, 1962).

[3]Robert H. Bremmer, *From the Depths: The Discovery of Poverty in the United States* (New York: New York University Press, 1956), esp. pp. 26-35, 41-42, 57-61, and Charles I. Foster, *An Errand of Mercy* (Chapel Hill: University of North Carolina Press, 1960).

[4]Timothy L. Smith, *Revivalism and Social Reform* (Nashville: Abingdon Press, 1957), esp. pp. 148-224.

[5]Clifford S. Griffin, *Their Brothers' Keepers: Moral Stewardship in the United States, 1800-1865* (New Brunswick, N. J.: Rutgers University Press, 1960), p. 48.

[6]Norris A. Magnuson, *Salvation in the Slums: Evangelical Social Welfare Work, 1865-1920* (Minneapolis) Ph.D. dissertation, Dept. of History, University of Minnesota, 1968.

[7]Timothy L. Smith, *Called unto Holiness: The Story of the Nazarenes* (Kansas City, Mo.: Nazarene Publishing House, 1962), esp. pp. 113-116, 200-203.

[8]*Ibid.*, p. 318.

[9]Magnuson, *op. cit.*

[10]Urban T. Holmes III, *The Future Shape of Ministry* (New York: Seabury Press, 1971), pp. 116-119.

[11]Brenda M. Meehan, "A. C. Dixon: An Early Fundamentalist," *Foundations,* Vol. X, No. 1 (January-March 1967), p. 53.

[12]*Ibid.*, pp. 53-55.

[13]Richard K. Curtis, *They Called Him Mister Moody* (Garden City, N.Y.: Doubleday, 1962), p. 266.

[14]*Ibid.*, pp. 266-267.

[15]*Ibid.*, p. 235.

[16]*Ibid.*, p. 267.

[17]William G. McLoughlin, Jr., *Billy Sunday Was His Real Name* (Chicago: University of Chicago Press, 1955).

[18]Harold J. Ockenga, "Evangelism and the Journey Outward," in George M. Wilson, ed., *Evangelism Now* (Minneapolis: World Wide Publications, 1970), p. 125. See also Bernard L. Ramm, *The Right, The Good, and the Happy* (Waco, Tex.: Word Books, 1971), pp. 127-132.

[19]Clifford V. Anderson, *The Christian and Social Concern* (Evanston, Ill.: Harvest Publications, 1971), pp. 23, 26.

[20]Richard V. Pierard, *The Unequal Yoke* (Philadelphia: J. B. Lippincott Co., 1970), pp. 29-37.

[21]Timothy L. Smith, "Revivalism and Social Reform," lecture at Bethel College and Seminary Faculty Retreat, September 5, 1962.

[22]The editor of *Christianity Today,* "Evangelicals in the Social Struggle," in Donald E. Hartsock, ed., *Contemporary Religious Issues* (Belmont, Calif.: Wadsworth Publishing Co., 1968), pp. 284-299.

[23]John Warwick Montgomery, "Evangelical Social Responsibility in Theological Perspective," Chap. 1 in Gary R. Collins, ed., *Our Society in Turmoil* (Carol Stream, Ill.: Creation House, 1970), p. 18.

[24]*Ibid.*, pp. 18-20.

[25]*Ibid.*, p. 22.

[26]*Ibid.*, pp. 22-23.

[27]See David O. Moberg, *Inasmuch: Christian Social Responsibility in the Twentieth Century* (Grand Rapids, Mich.: Eerdmans, 1965), pp. 17-22. See also John R. W. Stott, *Christ the Controversialist* (Downers Grove, Ill.: Inter-Varsity Press, 1970), pp. 179-191.

[28]Bruce L. Shelley, *Evangelicalism in America* (Grand Rapids, Mich.: Eerdmans, 1967), p. 116.

[29]See Richard Hofstadter, *Social Darwinism in American Thought, 1860-1915* (Philadelphia: University of Pennsylvania Press, 1945).

[30]Richard Hofstadter, *Anti-Intellectualism in American Life* (New York: Alfred A. Knopf, 1963), p. 134.

[31]*Ibid.*, pp. 118-119, 129-136, 140-141.

[32]Pierard, *op. cit.* See also Robert G. Clouse, Robert D. Linder, and Richard V. Pierard, eds., *Protest and Politics: Christianity and Contemporary Affairs* (Greenwood, S. C.: Attic Press, 1968).

[33]Mark Hatfield, *Conflict and Conscience* (Waco, Tex.: Word Books, 1971).

[34]This schematic pattern of reaction to new social issues represents a hypothesis to test more than the result of objective study. It grows out of personal observations pertinent to such issues as racial desegregation,

birth control, social security, capital punishment, medicare and medic-
aid, and the mental health movement. The lag of evangelicals in the
development of theological and ethical implications of new scientific
developments has been noted by Bernard Ramm, "Evangelical Theology and Technological Shock," *Journal of the American Scientific Affiliation,* Vol. XXIII, No. 2 (June 1971), pp. 52-56.

Do Evangelicals Lack Social Concern?   3

Evangelist Tom Skinner, in an address to the 1971 meeting of the American Baptist Convention, rebuked evangelical, Bible-believing Christians for their silence on social issues and their recent identification with the "hoot and cry" for law and order during the upsurge in black revolution and rebellion. Jesus, he said, was a revolutionary. He was arrested "because he was dangerous, and he was dangerous because he was changing the system."[1]

A widespread criticism of "conservative evangelicals" is that they are "so heavenly minded that they are of no earthly good." They are seen as offering "pie in the sky by and by" while hampering every effort to give people who lack "pie" in current society from receiving even a small piece in this life.[2]

These criticisms are not wholly without foundation. If religious institutions are divided into the two camps of (1) eternity-oriented and God-centered churches, which are concerned chiefly for the salvation of individual souls and ultimate rewards and penalties doled out in a life beyond the grave, and (2) morality-oriented and society-centered churches, which have a totally this-worldly social emphasis,[3] there can be no doubt as to the category into which evangelicals would place themselves. (The real world, of course, is not that simple. Most Christian groups probably fall somewhere between those two camps if we think of them as representing the two poles of a series of possibilities.) Evangelicals are more inclined toward otherworldly perspectives, while theological liberals give greater attention to conditions and needs of men in contemporary society.

The tensions that have arisen between these perspectives within the various Christian denominations constitute a major source of conflict and cleavage in Christendom today, as we saw in Chapter 1. The "news in religion" reports frequently carry stories based upon these divisions. The struggles involve untold hours of debate, committee work, and strategic maneuvering within religious bodies. They have led to the organization of many special-interest groups within most of the major denominations. They divert attention from numerous other matters of Christian concern.

The fundamentalist reaction to criticism of their otherworldliness by "scholars who equate technological advancement with spiritual growth and are thus illusioned into the false hope of ushering in a kingdom of righteousness without the bodily presence of the 'Servant of Righteousness'" is epitomized by this statement from a Bible school newsletter:

The scarecrow jargon of "being so heavenly minded as to be of no earthly good" has stifled in the hearts of many believers the wooings of the Spirit of God to "set their affections on things above, not on things on the earth." The warmth of evangelism has been eclipsed by the warps of ecumenism advocating world-encompassing "social gospel" projects which are sapping the very strength of the true gospel.[4]

On the other side of the conflict is a contrary position that calls for a "moratorium on preaching" and an emphasis upon producing social change in society. It holds that

The changing of the structures of society, and not the proclamation of a message to win converts, should be the true evangelistic burden of today's church.[5]

Major social action efforts have been introduced in recent years in the United Presbyterian Church, Episcopal Church, National Council of Churches, World Council of Churches, and other religious bodies. As a result, a backlash of major proportions has resulted in a "pocketbook revolt" on the part of many major contributors; members have moved out of their churches, and protest groups have been organized to combat the efforts of their denominations to change the structures of society by "financing revolution, supporting violence, inciting to civil disobedience" instead of trusting orderly change and "the potency of Christianity's age-old weapons —reconciliation and love—which over the ages have again and again transformed both men and their societies."[6] Conservative columnists analyze the problem as centering in preachers who have lost most of their religion and are seeking new "relevance" on picketlines or through "preaching overheated sermons based on dubious theories of economics and sociology" which turn people off. "Right now religion is in trouble again from the too-little-God disease."[7]

The ideological struggle between social actionist and traditional Christian perspectives is the subject of a growing body of social science research. The remainder of this chapter is devoted to a few representative studies, giving special attention to those which pertain to social concern among evangelicals.

The Gathering Storm

In his perceptive analysis of the widening gap between the clergy and laymen in American churches, Jeffrey K.

Do Evangelicals Lack Social Concern?

Hadden identified three important dimensions to "the gathering storm in the churches." All three—the crisis over the meaning and purpose for being of the church, the crisis of belief, and the power struggles related to the crisis of authority—are closely related to questions about the relationship of the church to social issues.

Herein lies perhaps the most important basis of conflict between clergy and laity: The clergyman's new theology has moved him beyond the four walls of the church and prompted him to express God's love in concern for the world, particularly the underprivileged, and in the desire to change the structures of society which have ascribed to many a lower and disadvantaged status in life. The layman, on the other hand, seeks comfort and escape from the world in the sanctuary of God. He does not understand why ministers are not satisfied to restrict their concern to their own fellowship of believers, and to the extent that clergymen move outside their own flock, they pursue a collision course with laity.[8]

Hadden's conclusion is based upon a broad range of evidence, not the least of which consists of survey data on the opinions of large samples of clergy and laity. The clergy data were gathered in 1965 by a questionnaire mailed to a random sample of 7,441 parish clergy in six major Protestant denominations (American Baptist, Episcopalian, American Lutheran, Missouri Synod Lutheran, Methodist, and Presbyterian U.S.A.). Among the 524 questions was a request for self-classification of theological position into one of six categories: fundamentalist, conservative, neo-orthodox, liberal, Universalist-Unitarian, other. Except for the Episcopalians, seventeen percent of whom chose "other" (usually writing in "Anglican" or "Anglican Catholic"), no more than two percent of the clergy from any denomination chose the latter two categories, so they were excluded from the analyses.

There were replies from 342 fundamentalists, 3,182 conservatives, 2,032 neo-orthodox, and 1,560 liberals.[9]

Sharp differences in political orientations were found between the fundamentalists and conservatives, on the one hand, and the neo-orthodox and liberals, on the other. (For the sake of convenience, the former will be identified here as "conservatives" and the latter as "liberals.") The conservatives were very strongly inclined toward the Republican Party, while the liberals were nearly evenly divided between Republican and Democratic preferences with a much heavier proportion (over one-fourth) independent. In contrast to the liberals, conservative theological orientations were associated with the belief that government is providing too many services that should be left to private enterprise, agreement that most people who live in poverty could do something about their situation if they really wanted to (fundamentalists agreeing more strongly than the other conservatives), support for Goldwater in the 1964 presidential election (especially strong among fundamentalists), and an unfaltering commitment to the free enterprise system as "the single economic system compatible with the requirements of personal freedom and constitutional government."[10] Theological position was found to be more important than age in predicting the attitudes indicated by eight civil rights items, theological conservatives being less sympathetic with the civil rights cause.[11] Among the laity, however, "biblical literalism," an indicator of fundamentalist belief, was unrelated to beliefs about government, free enterprise, and individual responsibility for poverty.[12]

A relationship observed between social status and political preferences suggests that there is a significant structural source of conflict between the clergy and laity in American Protestantism. The clergy who serve the congregations which have a preponderance of professional, managerial, and white-collar members are the most likely to hold liberal political perspectives, in contrast to the conservative political views of their parishioners; the clergy who serve predominantly blue-collar congregations are most likely to hold conservative political views, but blue-collar people are the most likely to be politically liberal. The dilemma grows in large part out of the fact that churches of high social status recruit ministers who have acquired a high-status and high-quality seminary education. Most such seminaries "have long traditions as centers of liberal theology and progressive political thought," so higher-status churches "are systematically hiring men who are politically more liberal than the constituency of the congregation."[13]

Research has demonstrated the possibility that church members tend to have political perspectives modified somewhat from those of other people with similar social characteristics in the direction of their ministers' views,[14] but it is possible that the ostensible tendency to change in that direction reflects a self-selection factor in which laity who are highly dissatisfied with their minister withdraw from the congregation or its activities. (In addition, questions about the research methods and findings make the findings more tentative than definitive.[15]) At any rate, we know that political issues often interfere with Christian fellowship.

Hadden recommends that the clergy be less dogmatic on some specific stands because social problems are extremely complex and ambiguous and that they work toward establishing general ethical principles rather than by responding on an *ad hoc* basis to every issue that arises.[16] The wind in the gathering storm may be harnessed in the sails of constructive church action if they will heed his advice.

Comfort or Challenge?

Another aspect of the storm that is raging within and among the churches relates to tensions about the basic purpose of the church. In their analysis of the beliefs of Episcopalian parishioners, priests, and bishops surveyed in 1952, Glock, Ringer, and Babbie found no relationship between members' attitudes toward social issues on which the Episcopal Church had taken an official stand and their degree of involvement in church life. They did, however, discover a rather sharp contrast between the clergy and laity on questions related to the purpose of the church and its role in public life. Seventy percent of the priests but only forty-six percent of the parishioners believed that it is proper for the church to state its position on political issues to the local, state, and national government. On every specific issue analyzed except that of partisan participation in political activity, the clergy were relatively more supportive than the lay members of the principle that their church has a responsibility for secular society, and their sociopolitical perspectives tended to be more clearly "liberal" than those of the laity. The intensity of church involvement of the members was not related to either the desire for withdrawal of the Episcopal Church from secular issues or to viewing the church as an instrument of social change.[17]

In general, these Episcopalians tended more than their clergy to view the basic function of the church as one of providing comfort, serving as a refuge for those denied access to valued achievements and rewards in everyday life, and providing personal comfort for deprivations experienced in secular society, while the clergy were more inclined than the parishioners to seek to abolish suffering rather than simply make it more bearable. This led Glock, Ringer, and Babbie to develop "the Marxian hypothesis" that church members who are deeply involved in the church reflect a sense of alienation from the world, a desire to escape from it through attachment to the church, a wish to have their church escape from the world with them, and hence a rejection of political activity by the church. Their partial test of the hypothesis provides evidence both in its support and in contradiction to it.[18]

If further research supports the Marxian hypothesis, scholars eventually may conclude that the religion against which Marxist atheists have been revolting is primarily that of an otherworldly fundamentalism. The proverbial aloofness of fundamentalists from direct involvement in most current social issues may be interpreted as evidence in support of Glock's deprivation theory, which sees the need for comfort as a major source of religious beliefs, as well as of the Marxian hypothesis. Rejection of the world, the attempt to escape from its trials and frustrations into the warmth of Christian fellowship, and a message emphasizing that the last shall be first and the despised of this earth shall be rulers in Christ's millennial Kingdom, all lend credence to Karl Marx's idea that "religion is the opiate of the people."[19]

Salvation and Compassion

Many Christians were shocked at findings reported by Milton Rokeach in the 1969 H. Paul Douglass Lectures sponsored by the Religious Research Association, for they concluded with this statement:

... the data presented here lead me to propose that man's relations to his fellowman will probably thrive at least a bit more if he altogether forgets or unlearns or ignores what organized religion has tried to teach him about values and what values are for.[20]

Christians generally have believed that their faith promotes loving concern for their fellow men and wholesome relationships with them, but Rokeach's research on a national sample of over 1,400 adult Americans did not support their opinion. The Rokeach Value Survey asks respondents to rank eighteen terminal values, which refer to preferred end-states of existence, in order of their perceived importance as guiding principles in daily life. The largest differences in terminal values were found in regard to the concept of *salvation*; Protestants ranked it fourth, Catholics thirteenth, and Jews and nonbelievers eighteenth. Jews ranked *a sense of accomplishment, equality, pleasure, family security, inner harmony,* and *wisdom* higher than did the other groups. Protestants ranked *a sense of accomplishment* lower than any other group, while Catholics ranked *equality* and *pleasure* lower and *national security* higher than the others.[21]

The Rokeach Value Survey also asks respondents to rank eighteen instrumental values, which pertain to preferred modes of behavior. The sharpest difference among the four religious categories of respondents was found for *forgiving,* which was ranked fourth by Protestants and Catholics, fifteenth by Jews, and sixteenth by nonbelievers. (*Honest* was ranked highest by all four groups; *ambitious* was second and *responsible* third among Protestants and Catholics, and they were ranked only slightly lower by Jews and others.) *Clean, obedient,* and *polite* were ranked highest by the Christians, next highest by Jews, and lowest by nonbelievers; *broadminded, independent,* and *intellectual* were ranked significantly higher by the latter two groups than by Protestants and Catholics.

Rokeach concluded that the values of *salvation* and *forgiving* stand out as the most distinctively Christian. *Salvation* also differentiated the most sharply among the six Protestant groups, Baptists ranking it third on the average, Lutherans ninth, Methodists tenth, Presbyterians and Congregationalists eleventh, and Episcopalians fourteenth. Christians who attended church frequently ranked both *salvation* and *forgiving* higher than those who attended rarely or never. Among a college-student sample, those who said their religion was important to them in everyday life ranked *salvation* in first place, while those who ranked it as of medium importance (on a seven-point scale) ranked it sixteenth, and those who ranked it low put *salvation* in the eighteenth place among the terminal values. The differences among the student rankings were not as pronounced for *forgiving,* but they were in the same direction (ranked sixth by those who perceived religion to be of high importance in daily life, twelfth by those who perceived it to be of medium importance, and thirteenth by those who gave it low importance).[22]

Having identified *salvation* and *forgiving* as the two values that are the most distinctively Christian, Rokeach then analyzed various attitudes toward Martin Luther King's assassination, civil rights, the poor, student protest, and church involvement in social issues. He found that on all but three of thirty-two issues, persons who never go to church were more compassionate than churchgoers; fourteen of the differences were statistically significant. (The three exceptions were nonsignificant.) Those who placed high value upon *salvation* were rather consistently less compassionate than others, but the value placed upon *forgiving* did not relate consistently to most of the items.

The general picture that emerges from the results presented
... is that those who place a high value on *salvation* are
conservative, anxious to maintain the *status quo,* and un-
sympathetic or indifferent to the plight of the black and the
poor. . . . Considered all together, the data suggest a portrait of
the religious-minded as a person having a self-centered preoc-
cupation with saving his own soul, an other-worldly orientation
coupled with an indifference toward or even a tacit endorsement
of a social system that would perpetuate social inequality and
injustice.[23]

Rokeach concluded that, if Christian values do serve as
standards of conduct, they seem to be employed more
often to guide man's conduct away from rather than
toward his fellow man, as standards for condemning
others, or to guide rationalization rather than as standards
to judge oneself or guide one's own conduct. This seems
incompatible with the comp ssion taught in the Sermon
on the Mo nt and suggests a deeply embedded hypocrisy
within many religiously oriented individuals as well as
within organized religion as a social institution.[24]

Rebuttal and Reaffirmation

Rokeach's lectures brought an immediate response from
the audience which lasted many months. In order to give
both him and his critics an equitable opportunity for
constructive dialogue, I arranged for a series of critical
reviews by representatives of four pertinent disciplines in
the *Review of Religious Research,* of which I was editor.
The critics pointed to problems in the research methodol-
ogy, implicit assumptions underlying the study, linguis-
tic problems in the two lists of values, theoretical difficulties, interpretative ambiguities, qualifications of the
implications for action, and the need for further study of
numerous significant issues raised. In summary, these
critiques indicate that many of Rokeach's conclusions

must be treated with appropriate reservations and qualifications.[25]

The temptation by churchmen—especially those who
place a high value upon *salvation!*—is therefore to ignore
Rokeach's findings and conclusions. To do so would be a
serious mistake, for, as Rodney Stark indicated in his
evaluation, other studies using different methodological
approaches have produced findings that are very similar.[26]

Some of this evidence comes from the work of Stark
and Glock. For example, in a study which used 1963 data
from church members in northern California they found
that the proportion who scored high on their measure of
ethicalism fell systematically from the more liberal
Protestant denominations to those that are theologically
conservative. (The only exception was the "small Protestant sects" whose members revealed the highest proportion of high scores on ethicalism. Their variation from the
general pattern was explained by their belief that everything has relevance to salvation.[27]) In other words, the
more conservative a Protestant group is, the less it tends
to be concerned about ethical values. Among Roman
Catholics, however, persons higher on ethicalism were
somewhat more likely to be highly orthodox than those
who were low, presumably because of the emphasis in
Catholicism upon the social responsibilities of the Christian.

Their findings led the authors to conclude that "there
seems to be little long-term future for the church as we
know it," for the more ethically concerned church members were, the more likely they were to be liberal in other
respects. Many studies indicate that members who are
theologically liberal participate less in the church and
give it weaker support than those with "high orthodoxy,"
and they also have lower levels of private devotional

activities, the experiential aspects of religion, religious knowledge, and particularism (the belief that only Christians can be saved). Assuming that the institutional church is predicated on traditional theological concepts, they noted how it lost its hold on members when such concepts became outmoded. In the search for relevant ethics concerned for creation of a humane society, people shift away from the orthodox bodies into liberal ones; then from the latter they drop out entirely from the church. Ethics therefore may be the death of the church, although not necessarily of religion.[28]

Elsewhere in their report, however, Stark and Glock indicate that "Among Protestants, ethicalism is virtually unrelated to any other aspect of religiousness" and only weakly, though negatively, related to orthodoxy, ritual, knowledge, and communal involvement. Hence concern for man-to-man ethics is not part of a general Protestant religious commitment. People with an ethical orientation are more likely to be deterred than challenged by what they find in church. The more one is committed to ethicalism, the less likely he is to participate actively in church life and to contribute financially to it. The greater the extent to which members have accepted the ethical preachments of Christianity, the more they seem inclined to treat the church as irrelevant.[29]

There is a serious flaw, however, in the Ethicalism Index. It is a composite of answers to only two items, "Doing good for others" and "Loving thy neighbor," each of which is to be classified as "absolutely necessary for salvation" (two points each), "probably would help in gaining salvation" (one point), or "probably has no influence on salvation" (no points). The total score therefore can vary from 0 for rejecting both items to 4 for holding both to be absolutely necessary for salvation.[30]

Do Evangelicals Lack Social Concern?

Every Christian who is consistent with the teachings of the New Testament, at least as they are interpreted by evangelicals, would of necessity have a score of 0 if the statements are taken at face value because he knows that salvation is a gift of God that cannot be earned; it has been earned for all by Jesus Christ. The statistical relationships resulting from Stark and Glock's Ethicalism Index therefore are invalid and unreliable, at least for theologically conservative Protestants. Nevertheless, thirty-seven percent of the Missouri Synod Lutherans and thirty-three percent of the Southern Baptists had scores of four. This suggests that many respondents may have adapted to the questions that had an inadequate number of alternative response categories by concluding that, since faith without works is dead, the presence of works which are "the fruit of salvation" is evidence of salvation and therefore is "absolutely necessary."

If the studies by Rokeach and Stark and Glock were the only ones bearing on the subject, evangelicals might be able to lean back and say that the evidence on the lack of social compassion among theological conservatives is so weak that it can be ignored. Only by blinding their eyes to a rapidly expanding body of factual knowledge could they take such a position.

Social Concern and Religious Liberalism

Further evidence of the relative lack of social concern among evangelicals and other theologically conservative Christians has emerged from many sociological studies. We will present only a few examples of results from the steadily expanding body of knowledge on the subject.

Lawrence L. Kersten's research on clergy and laity in four Lutheran denominations included a Social Welfare Index combining responses to four items. He found that clergymen with liberal theological beliefs were much more likely than conservatives to take a liberal stand regarding social welfare. The differences were smaller among laymen, but the less knowledge they had of the Bible, the more liberal were their views on welfare. "The results suggest that a conservative social philosophy may emanate from biblical knowledge."[31] Of course, it is possible that generational differences are an intervening variable; if older people know the Bible better and also are more conservative about social welfare, the observed relationships may be due to age differences rather than to Bible knowledge as such.

The theologically more conservative clergy were more hawkish than theological liberals in their attitudes toward war, and they also were more likely to express anti-Semitic attitudes, more opposed to the expansion of civil liberties, more approving of harsh punishment for deviants (convicted murderers, sex offenders, and homosexuals), more inclined to believe that premarital sex will lead to serious emotional difficulties, more opposed to the legalization of abortion, more opposed to congressional restrictions on the sale of guns, and more favorable to traditional Lutheran views on the roles of the laity, women, the clergy, and the congregation. Kersten discovered that the clergy on the liberal side of the liberal-conservative continuum answered an average of ninety-one percent of all issues with liberal responses and that conservatives also tended to be consistent in their attitudinal pattern. The differences among Lutheran laymen tended to be in the same direction but were not as sharply differentiated, so most were not statistically significant.

Since humane treatment of one's fellow men is a core characteristic of what Kersten labeled as "liberal" perspectives, it can be concluded that conservative religious beliefs among Lutherans tend to be associated with less humane orientations toward other people.

Religion and Prejudice

The research that has found a relationship between religious conservatism, prejudice, and lack of social compassion for minorities and culturally deprived people in society must be taken with considerable reservation at this time. The research itself has flaws; with greater refinement and sophistication certain aspects of the tendencies may be reversed. We know, for example, that the relationship between religious commitment and prejudice is not direct or linear but curvilinear; that is, the least prejudice is found among both the most and the least religious people, and the greatest amount occurs among those who are nominally religious.[32] Since churches include a large proportion of nominal Christians, the impression is given when members are compared with nonmembers (who tend to be the "least religious") that the members are more prejudiced. But the devout among them are not!

Through factor analysis Bernard Spilka and James F. Reynolds found that the concept of God held by people is related to prejudice. Those who hold prejudiced views are more likely to see God as unreal, impersonal, abstract, distant, and inaccessible, but those who interpret God as concerned, considerate, kind, and personally involved and interested in the affairs of men have ideas and feelings that are more consistent with the Golden Rule and human brotherhood.[33] Relationships between religious conservatism and prejudice also are attenuated when such variables as education, social class, and anomie (normlessness or the inability to fit one's normative system to a situation as experienced) are controlled.[34]

Measuring instruments used to study religion and prejudice may also contaminate the results. The powerful relationship between "religion and anti-Semitism" found by Glock and Stark,[35] for example, is due almost entirely to defining the Christian religion in terms of a Religious Bigotry Index, which itself is contaminated by anti-Semitic content.[36] It is likely that different criteria of religiosity and divergent patterns of church activity and belief represent different "types" of religion and that this accounts for discrepant findings about relationships between religion and prejudice.[37]

Conclusions

Evangelicals as well as theological liberals vary widely in their perspectives toward other people. In some current research in which I am involved, for example, we are finding that many church members who adhere strongly to evangelical beliefs also are very "liberal" in their perspectives toward blacks, welfare recipients, and members of other socioeconomic minorities and ethnic subcultures. Preliminary findings of the Study of Generations project involving a scientific national cross-section of 4,745 members from the three largest Lutheran denominations in the United States also have demonstrated that Christian orthodoxy leads to less racial and religious prejudice rather than more.[38]

It is likely that further research will reveal that the current simplistic generalization that "religious people are more prejudiced" is a result of inadequate conceptual specification. Especially serious is the failure to discriminate between nominal church members who are merely "culturally religious" in order to meet the American social demand that everyone belong to some religious group or who use their religion for other extrinsic or consensual reasons and those members who hold solidly based faith commitments which are intrinsic to all of life, viewing their faith as generic to all of their activities and decisions. Nominal or extrinsic Christians apparently are more prejudiced than both humanists who profess to hold no religious faith and people who have sincere intrinsic faith commitments.[39] Evangelicals obviously idealize the latter category, although it must be recognized that evangelical congregations, like others, include both extrinsic and intrinsic members.

In view of the tendency of most research to find a relationship between conservative theology and a lack of social concern, the findings of a study by Thomas C. Campbell and Yoshio Fukuyama of 8,549 members of the United Church of Christ were surprising. Their purposive samples of major segments of the denomination indeed supported their hypotheses that the religious orientations of privileged persons reflect dominant cultural values, while those who are socially deprived have religious orientations which compensate for their deprivation. But they also found that people who were devotionally oriented, practicing personal pieties of daily devotional prayer and Bible reading as necessary parts of the Christian life, were more likely than others to accept Negroes socially and expressed greater sympathy for civil rights issues.[40]

Personal Christian commitment can support an active social concern.

Notes

[1]"U. S. Needs Black for President in 1972, Baptist Convention Told," *Minneapolis Star*, May 15, 1971, p. 9A.

[2]These criticisms may be less common among people in general than critical spokesmen imply. To my knowledge, no research has explored

the images and opinions about "evangelicals," "fundamentalists," and similar ideological faith groupings among representative samples of the American population. Until such research has been done, speculative statements of opinion will predominate in the discussions of evangelicals and their critics.

[3]This typology is developed in Paul H. Landis, *Social Control* (Philadelphia: J. B. Lippincott, rev. ed., 1956), pp. 212-220.

[4]"Is This the Year?" *VBI Vision,* Vol. IV, No. 7 (July 1967), p. 1.

[5]Quoted as the crux of the controversy by C. Peter Wagner, "Evangelism and Social Action in Latin America," *Christianity Today,* Vol. X, No. 7 (January 7, 1966), p. 10.

[6]Clarence W. Hall, "Must Our Churches Finance Revolution?" *Reader's Digest,* Vol. L (October 1971), p. 100.

[7]Jenkin Lloyd Jones, "Trouble in the Churches," *St. Paul Sunday Pioneer Press,* June 28, 1970, Section 2, p. 3.

[8]Jeffrey K. Hadden, *The Gathering Storm in the Churches* (Garden City, N. Y.: Doubleday and Co., 1969), p. 99.

[9]*Ibid.,* pp. 73-74.

[10]*Ibid.,* pp. 73-90.

[11]*Ibid.,* p. 118.

[12]*Ibid.,* p. 95.

[13]*Ibid.,* p. 85.

[14]See the studies of Benton Johnson: "Ascetic Protestantism and Political Preference," *Public Opinion Quarterly,* Vol. XXVI (Spring 1962), pp. 35-46; "Ascetic Protestantism and Political Preference in the Deep South," *American Journal of Sociology,* Vol. LXIX (January 1964), pp. 359-366; "Theology and Party Preference Among Protestant Clergymen," *American Sociological Review,* Vol. XXXI (April 1966), pp. 200-208.

[15]Gene F. Summers *et al.,* "Ascetic Protestantism and Political Preference: A Re-examination," *Review of Religious Research,* Vol. XII, No. 1 (Fall 1970), pp. 17-25.

[16]Hadden, *op. cit.,* pp. 234-235.

[17]Charles Y. Glock, Benjamin B. Ringer, and Earl R. Babbie, *To Comfort and to Challenge: A Dilemma of the Contemporary Church* (Berkeley: University of California Press, 1967), pp. 119-136, *passim.*

[18]*Ibid.,* pp. 126, 133-134.

[19]*Ibid.,* pp. 210-212. (Personally, I believe that the abuses associated with a politically established religion were more basic causes of the communist reaction against Christianity.)

[20]Milton Rokeach, "The H. Paul Douglass Lectures for 1969: Part I. Value Systems in Religion. Part II. Religious Values and Social Compassion," *Review of Religious Research,* Vol. XI (Fall 1969), pp. 3-39 (quotation from p. 37).

[21]*Ibid.,* pp. 5-6.

Do Evangelicals Lack Social Concern?

[22] *Ibid.*, pp. 6-21.

[23] *Ibid.*, p. 29.

[24] *Ibid.*, pp. 35-37.

[25] David O. Moberg *et al.*, "Religious Values and Social Compassion: A Critical Review of the 1969 H. Paul Douglass Lectures by Dr. Milton Rokeach," *Review of Religious Research,* Vol. XI (Winter 1970), pp. 136-162.

[26] Rodney Stark, "Rokeach, Religion, and Reviewers: Keeping an Open Mind," in *ibid.*, pp. 151-154.

[27] Rodney Stark and Charles Y. Glock, *American Piety: The Nature of Religious Commitment* (Berkeley: University of California Press, 1969), pp. 69-76, 181-182.

[28] Rodney Stark and Charles Y. Glock, "Will Ethics Be the Death of Christianity?" *Trans-Action,* Vol. V, No. 7 (June 1968), pp. 7-14. This conclusion focuses upon the movement of people from sectarian religious groups into more conventional churches, from these into liberal groups, and from them into the "nonchurch" population. It overlooks the fact that many people are converted out of the liberal and nonchurch groups and move into sectarian and evangelical groups, thus helping to replenish the stream.

[29] Stark and Glock, *American Piety,* pp. 181-182, 216-220.

[30] *Ibid.*, p. 71.

[31] Lawrence L. Kersten, *The Lutheran Ethic: The Impact of Religion on Laymen and Clergy* (Detroit: Wayne State University Press, 1970), p. 64. His Religious Knowledge Index is based upon nine items.

[32] Robin Williams, Jr., *Strangers Next Door* (Englewood Cliffs, N. J.: Prentice-Hall, 1964).

[33] Bernard Spilka and James F. Reynolds, "Religion and Prejudice: A Factor-Analytic Study," *Review of Religious Research,* Vol. VI, No. 3 (Spring 1965), pp. 163-168.

[34] James J. Vanecko, "Religious Behavior and Prejudice: Some Dimensions and Specifications of the Relationship," *Review of Religious Research,* Vol. VIII, No. 1 (Fall 1966), pp. 27-37, and James J. Vanecko, "Types of Religious Behavior and Levels of Prejudice," *Sociological Analysis,* Vol. XXVIII, No. 3 (Fall 1969), pp. 111-122.

[35] Charles Y. Glock and Rodney Stark, *Christian Beliefs and Anti-Semitism* (New York: Harper & Row, 1966).

[36] W. R. Heinz, "The Fundamentalist Anti-Semite," *Trans-Action,* Vol. IV, No. 9 (1967), pp. 76-77.

[37] Bernard Spilka, "Research on Religious Beliefs: A Critical Review," Chap. 13 in Merton P. Strommen, ed., *Research on Religious Development: A Comprehensive Handbook* (New York: Hawthorn Books, 1971), p. 502.

[38] "First Study of Generations Results Revealed," *Publication of Youth Research Center,* Vol. III, No. 3 (Fall 1971), pp. 1-3.

[39]These generalizations are based largely upon Gordon W. Allport and J. M. Ross, "Personal Religious Orientation and Prejudice," *Journal of Personality and Social Psychology,* Vol. V, No. 4 (1967), pp. 432-443, and Russell O. Allen and Bernard Spilka, "Committed and Consensual Religion: A Specification of Religion-Prejudice Relationships," *Journal for the Scientific Study of Religion,* Vol. VI, No. 2 (Fall 1967), pp. 191-206. See also James E. Dittes, "Religion, Prejudice, and Personality," with Appendix by Dwight W. Culver, Chap. 9 in Merton P. Strommen, ed., *Research on Religious Development: A Comprehensive Handbook* (New York: Hawthorn Books, 1971), pp. 355-390.

[40]Thomas C. Campbell and Yoshio Fukuyama, *The Fragmented Layman: An Empirical Study* (Philadelphia: Pilgrim Press, 1970).

The Sociological Analysis of Evangelism

A businessman waited with me for the departure of an airport limousine in South Bend, Indiana, when I was on my way to the Faith and Order Colloquium at Notre Dame University in 1967. He inquired where I was going and then responded to my explanation somewhat apologetically, saying that, although he had been reared in the Congregational Church, he was no longer a church member. Then he made this significant comment: "If the faiths can get together on evangelism, they can get together on anything." I tend to agree; the issues related to evangelism strike at the very heart of the churches' nature, mission, methods, and relationships to the world.

Dealing with evangelism as a sociologist and "as an outsider from the inside" (that is, as one who is not a denominational administrator but who is a church member), I could easily mix my roles of Christian layman and social scientist. The relative dearth of systematic sociological research on this subject also introduces important hazards. Let me, therefore, first of all clarify the social science frame of reference.

The Sociological Approach to Evangelism

The sociologist of religion can play a very significant role in the work of the churches. As a social scientist, his chief concern is to develop and test generalizations that will apply to a wide variety of individual cases, situations, and circumstances. When he deals with a topic like evangelism, he therefore develops hypotheses which grow out of social science theory and the findings or implications of research already done in related areas of study.[1]

Scientific hypotheses are generalizations to test. The true social scientist does not attempt to *prove* that his hypotheses are true, but he instead seeks all available pertinent evidence to *test* whether a given hypothesis may be accepted as tentatively verified or must be rejected on the basis of the evidence. In other words, the sociologist does not simply stack up evidence on one side of a subject he studies. Instead he deliberately attempts to discover negative instances and other contrary facts as well. (In that regard, he is more honest than those evangelists and ministers who make sweeping generalizations about mankind on the basis of a few casual illustrations.)

Most sociologists are very impatient with "common-sense" observations, no matter how firmly such opinions are entrenched within religious, governmental, or other groups as a result of long-term conditioning, formal education, repetition of clichés, the mass media of communications, and other institutional and interpersonal influences. They want to have "hard facts" rather than "soft-core opinions." They are hesitant about making statements of opinion on such unconventional topics, sociologically speaking, as evangelism unless they can support the opinions with theoretical or empirical evidence gleaned from research on it or related topics. They recognize that an oft-repeated error may be believed by multitudes but that it is error nevertheless. Any evangelistic program designed to reach them for the church or to use them in the service of the church must recognize that this skepticism is built into the very nature of their profession and thus into their *Weltanschauung* and self-conceptions.

The Sociological Analysis of Evangelism

In his role as a social scientist, the sociologist cannot originate values, goals, and ends. The basic values that guide human conduct must come from outside the sciences, with theology playing a major role. This does not mean, however, that sociology as such cannot play a part in directing social behavior. Action-oriented social research can help to discover the consequences of alternative institutional structures and programs. Evaluation research can disclose the latent (hidden, indirect, unintended) as well as the manifest (obvious, planned, intended) results of social organizations and processes. Experiments with various forms of evangelism accompanied by careful research could help to reveal which kinds are the most effective for which types of people. What reaches some in a given kind of social milieu may be totally useless in a different situation or may even have a negative impact upon other persons from the same environment. By helping to identify the numerous consequences of various alternatives, the sociologist can help to guide church action. Final decisions will still depend heavily upon nonsociological values, for each of the relative advantages and disadvantages likely to result from implementing a decision must be evaluated as to importance; the sociological input is but one of the bases for decision-making. Currently, however, it is much too neglected in Christian circles.

The following hunches about evangelism are expressed in the form of hypotheses. In order to be researchable, additional sharpening and careful operational definitions of their key concepts would be required. Here, however, they may be viewed as a series of impressions, guesses, opinions, and casual observations by one sociologist who recognizes their tenuous nature and the need for systematic research on all of them.

The Great Reversal

Some Hypotheses about Evangelism

1. *There is widespread confusion about the definition of evangelism* among all except fundamentalist and "conservative evangelical" Christians. A wide variety of activities is included by various religious groups under the heading of evangelism. These range all the way from traditional revivalistic efforts to social ministries, administration and reception of the sacraments, fellowship, the church school, worship, recreational activities, church-sponsored bowling leagues, small-group discussions, studying the community, social action, and casual personal contacts and friendships of church members. What one group identifies as evangelism is totally excluded from evangelism by another. Some argue that everything done by a Christian person or by a church congregation has evangelistic implications. But does this make all of their activities evangelism?

It is impossible for a social scientist to study what cannot be identified. If theologians and church administrators cannot agree on the definition of evangelism, operational definitions of evangelism developed by social scientists for research purposes are likely to prove unsatisfying or frustrating to men of action.

If evangelism is a product or effect more than an activity or program, the definition must be in terms of tangible results. In that event, sociologists can check the results to see which programs are and which are not in fact evangelistic. They may discover that a type of "negative evangelism" is often in operation in Christian churches. By this I mean that certain types of people may be repulsed or driven away from the church by the very same "evangelistic activities" that attract others.

In an interview survey of forty-six religious leaders and

scholars in a study of evangelism in 1953 we found that two polar types of religious conversion were identifiable with a continuum of variations in between. *The event definition* saw conversion as an instantaneous, miraculous experience of birth into the family of God, although it was recognized by all who held to that view that this event may be preceded by a lengthy preconversion process and that it ought to be followed by a process of Christian growth and development. *The process interpretation* of conversion saw it as a definite place of departure, point of turning, or beginning rather than as a separate, final act. Yet this point of turning or beginning could also be interpreted as a specific event, so the distinctions between these two groups may be largely a result of different emphases or of misinterpretation and misunderstanding. Differences in evangelistic methods were associated with the event and the process types of definition, although the precise words used to define conversion varied widely. We concluded:

To what extent these differences and the cleavages in Christian circles related to them are a result of semantic differences and a lack of sympathetic understanding of slight variations between their viewpoints and those of others we did not try to determine. Superficially, at least, it appears that the various Protestant groups with their different emphases have much more in common with respect to their beliefs about religious conversion than most of them in their sectarian biases would care to admit.[2]

It is likely that, despite the progress of dialogue and the ecumenical movement since 1953, there are even more disparate interpretations of conversion today and hence at least as much disagreement about evangelism as there was at that time. Some interpret evangelism as saving people's lives for their earthly existence, while others see it as winning souls for the hereafter. Some conceive of it as the simple addition of new church members, while others view it in terms of baptisms or confirmations. For some, evangelism means convincing people of the validity of a given set of folkways, mores, or institutional structures, while others interpret it as helping God's children (whom they consider to be all people) respond to God. Hiding such differences by pretending they do not exist may help to accentuate their negative emotional impact upon people; bringing them out into the open is a first step toward resolving them or at least tolerating them sympathetically. An important second step is sociological research to reveal the extent to which, and groups by which, they are held; the strength of such convictions; and their social implications. Obviously, theological studies also are of great significance to this topic.

2. *The language used to describe evangelism has significant consequences.* If the originator of a communication has a different definition of a basic term from that of its receiver, true communication may be impossible. In ecumenical contexts semantic problems become especially important, for each party involved in a discussion may believe effective communication is occurring when in fact it is not. Consider the impression conveyed by each of the following terms sometimes used to label evangelistic programs or as synonyms, cognates, or equivalents of "evangelism":

Witnessing	The apostolate
Revival meetings	Church extension
Proselyting	Membership recruitment
Crusade for Christ	Redeeming society
Restructuring the social order	Making converts
Church renewal	Winning converts
Church membership campaign	Securing Christian commitment
Soul-winning	Proclamation of the Gospel
Missions	Annunciation

It is likely that each conveys a somewhat different picture to your mind. Each is likely to have somewhat different emotional overtones. The use of any one of them is likely to impart much more than a strictly objective picture of specific action. The response will be in terms of the total image in the mind, and this image will differ widely from members of one reference group to those of another. Great variations may accompany denominational differences as well as social class contrasts and distinctions between theologians, pastors, other clergymen, lay church leaders, run-of-the-mill church members, inactive members, non-church members who are friendly to the church, and antagonistic nonmembers. The label used to designate an evangelistic effort may therefore have important implications for its effectiveness as well as for relationships with members of other religious groups. These differential images, interpretations, and impacts deserve behavioral science research.

3. *Theological differences pertinent to the nature of salvation and the means by which it is attained are a major source of division.* Max Weber, the great German sociologist, pointed out that "world images" created by ideas have often been like switchmen determining

the tracks along which action has been pushed by the dynamic of interest. "From what" and "for what" one wished to be redeemed and, let us not forget, "could be" redeemed, depended upon one's image of the world.[3]

Among the many such possibilities, Weber mentioned the wish to be saved from political and social servitude to a Messianic realm in the future of this world; from being defiled by ritual impurity to a hope for the pure beauty of psychic and bodily existence; from the play of human passions to the quietude of the pure beholding of the divine; from radical evil and the servitude of sin to hope for eternal, free benevolence in the lap of a fatherly god; from barriers to the finite expressed in suffering, misery, death, and the threatening punishment of hell to hope for eternal bliss in a future existence; or from senseless brooding and events to longing for dreamless sleep.[4] To these may be added other desires and beliefs evident in Christian evangelism. The goal cultivated by evangelistic programs or sought by those who are evangelized may be redemption from a deviant, neurotic mentality to the stability of a normal mind; from rejecting Christ to a life committed to Him; from being an enemy of God to being His friend; from a life of sin to a life of righteousness; from political and moral corruption or national decline to patriotic loyalty and "true Americanism"; from serving Satan to serving God; from selfishness to concern for others; from personal failure to social or psychic success; from an "incomplete and empty" life to one of satisfaction and fullness. There are numerous other possibilities, the verbal and social expressions of which are subject to sociological analysis.

The means of attaining salvation seem to vary considerably among Christian groups. If a denomination interprets man as made in the image of God and a spiritual child of God regardless of his personal response to God's claims upon him, its evangelism will differ greatly from that of the group that sees man as fallen into sin and redeemed by Jesus Christ only upon a personal acceptance of His vicarious atonement. Both will differ from the group that believes saving grace is bestowed through sacraments of baptism and communion.

It is possible that out of current changes in the ecclesiastical scene a new and basic cleavage will replace the present diversity of Christian groups. Perhaps Christians will be divided into those who believe Christ's redemption is conferred upon men through sacraments and those who believe it comes by faith alone through non-sacramental channels. Some nonsacramentalists tend to view the administration of the sacraments (presumably in contrast to their own "ordinances") as not significantly different from primitive magic. A few lay people, in fact, refer to the "hocus pocus of the Catholic Mass" in the same manner as they might refer to the "hocus pocus" of a magician performing at a children's party. Sacramentalists, in turn, tend to look with disdain upon their benighted brethren. Concepts of the clergy, priesthood, and ordination, of the nature and forms of worship, and of evangelism itself hinge to a considerable extent upon this basic theological difference.

Semantic problems also intrude into this issue. The term "sacrament" probably bears considerably different denotations and connotations among Roman Catholics from those of Methodists, and these in turn differ in meaning among those Baptists who use the word. Diverse meanings given to the same words by different religious groups help to confound the theological issues and make it more difficult for social scientists to study pertinent topics. Nevertheless, the sociologist can help to identify the differences between groups which are related to divergent interpretations of such topics as who (God, the church, the minister, etc.) saves whom (sinners, the world, society, Christians, church members, the baptized, believers, etc.), how (sacramentally or nonsacramentally, by personal response or by the actions of others, etc.), from what (sin, self, social disorganization, mental illness, etc.) and with what effects (this-worldly or otherworldly, personal or social, etc.). While ultimate theological questions cannot be answered thus, descriptive studies of the beliefs, believers, social implications, and the like can help men to relate themselves to one another more effectively as well as to determine to what extent their observable religious goals are being implemented.

4. *Differences in the goals of evangelism help to divide Christians.* Is the goal the "making of Christians"? If so, is it for their earthly welfare now or for heavenly rewards in a future life? Is it the building of an earthly institutional church, of a millennial Kingdom of God, or of a future Kingdom "eternal in the heavenlies"? Is it the changing of attitudes and beliefs or the changing of behavior? Is it the securing of individualistic personal commitments or the modification of social group orientations? Is it getting "souls" baptized or seeking the baptism of the Holy Spirit? Is it getting people to join a church or persuading them to make a deeper personal commitment to Christ? Is it moving to a higher level of well-being or a psychological compensation for deprivation? Is it reducing the incidence of social problems or alleviating feelings of anxiety in the minds of people? Is it the extension of American middle-class moral values or the propagation of spiritual principles for peace of mind? Is it spiritual and eternity-centered or earthly and morality-centered? Is it the primary goal of the Christian church or an inevitable by-product of *kerygma, diakonia,* and *koinonia?* The list could be extended almost *ad infinitum.* Most groups would deny the dichotomies, but they would probably fall closer to one extreme of each than to the other.

Furthermore, are the targets of evangelistic activity persons, groups, or social structures? If persons, must they be only those who have never been baptized, or those who are inactive in any church or religion, or those whose religious heritage is non-Christian, or those whose background lies in one's own denomination? Or, on the contrary, are the targets all who lack a personal commitment to Jesus Christ, even if they already are baptized or church members? Is proselytism, commonly called "sheep stealing" by clergymen, sanctioned, condoned, or condemned?

If the targets are social structures, to what extent is their consensus within the religious group on the proximate as well as the ultimate goals of social change?

What priority does evangelism have in the relative ranking of the church's ministries? How does it compare with religious education, worship, social and recreational activities, Bible study, other adult education, social ministries, social action, community leadership, and the like? Is it a major goal sought by the church or a minor subsidiary objective pursued only halfheartedly?

It is obvious to any careful observer of the American church scene that all of these issues create divisions within church congregations and denominations as well as between them. The extent to which these differences are present, their salience for the ongoing life of churches as social institutions, their intensity and relevance to the effectiveness of churches in fulfilling their avowed mission, and their role in religious conflict all deserve sociological research.

When the church's goals for evangelism are diffused or are poorly communicated to the clergy and laymen who are doing evangelistic work, the results are likely to be discouraging. On the other hand, goals that are unrealistically narrow may be attained easily but may lack enduring results.

5. *Evangelism typically fails to adapt its methods to fit the great variety of people and of human needs present in pluralistic society.* Direct evangelistic efforts often seem to assume that identical programs, approaches, appeals, techniques, and content may be used effectively for all

men and women. This ignores the great diversity of people in modern society with its complex division of labor, broad extent of opportunities for the expression of differences, and wide range of varieties of unbelief.[5] Individual and group differences are maximized in the contemporary free world, so it is realistic to expect that evangelistic approaches must be adjusted to fit their audiences if the evangelism is to be very effective.

Perhaps the middle-class domination and nature of American Christianity is a product of evangelism and church programs which assume that middle-class needs, middle-class methods, and middle-class objectives are the needs, methods, and objectives of all people. If so, it is not surprising that both the poor and the wealthy tend to be alienated from our churches. When church-type institutional activities are upheld as the normative ideal by religious leaders, they should not be amazed when they find that lower-class people, whose religious interests tend to be sect-type, either do not join their congregations or gradually drop out of them.[6] Although race remains one of the great dividers of Christians, social class may be an even greater one.[7]

6. *Pluralism in evangelism has functional consequences.* Not only do I refer to the diversity of programs mentioned above, but there is an analogy between the religious and the economic situation. American society has a type of "free enterprise" in religion that promotes competition between religious groups. If a Protestant congregation does not have a viable program, newcomers to the community and even members tend to drift into its competitors. This compels the clergy and lay leaders to provide, to a considerable degree, what people desire. These desires differ, however, among people of differ-

ent social class, ethnic and racial origin, educational level, occupation, regional background, and other characteristics. Self-selection of church membership is part of the reason for differences between congregations, but it is also partly an effect of these differences. Hence almost anyone can find a congregation that meets his interests, expectations, and needs. Competition thus contributes to the diversity of evangelistic and other church programs, and this, in turn, helps to increase the total number of church members in the nation.

If, as a result of cross-denominational church mergers and other successes of the ecumenical movement, a single evangelistic approach were to become dominant, it is conceivable that some of the functional effects of religious competition would be lost.[8] The same could be true if institutional strength became the basic end of the churches instead of a means toward other ends related to loving and serving God and man. For a society with voluntary church membership, the United States has a very high level of religiosity as measured by that dubious indicator. One of the factors that helps account for this is the pluralism of evangelistic endeavors and the accompanying competitive spirit that keeps church groups alert, active, and aggressive.

7. *The ultimate effectiveness of any evangelistic program depends upon the sincerity and intensity of personal Christian commitment among lay church members.* Even in our "mass society," personal influence remains very important. In the area of religion, it seems to have greater significance than published materials, formalized training courses, radio, television, and other media of mass communications. The nonverbal witness of laymen must, of course, be supplemented by verbal witness, for

Christian "faith comes from what is heard, and what is heard comes by the preaching of Christ" (Rom. 10:17). But just as indirect personal influences bear great significance in political decision-making,[9] we may hypothesize that they do also in religious decision-making.

The negative role of "hypocrisy" in evangelism is a factor in this as well. To my knowledge, it has never been studied sociologically, although the related topic of discrepancies between ideals and actualities has received some attention.

It is probable that mass evangelism is effective only when it is a culmination of personal influences. The deliberate personal cultivation of prospective Billy Graham Crusade converts and the significant role of friendships in the conversion process are indirect evidences in support of the thesis that people are more effective in reaching other people in conventional Christian evangelism than are impersonal materials and programs. The program, of course, can greatly help to stimulate, encourage, educate, and guide laymen in this task, but typically it is only the most deeply committed who are likely to take advantage of available impersonal resources.

Christian commitment which has an effective evangelistic impact seems usually, perhaps always, to be linked closely with group participation. Indeed, it can be questioned whether effective evangelism can ever occur apart from warm, accepting groups into which those who are evangelized can be assimilated.

Other Areas of Investigation

While the above hypotheses are not all in sharply scientific form, they do indicate certain topics about which factual evidence can be collected and analyzed by social scientists and religious researchers. They may seem no different from common-sense observations, and perhaps they are not at all unique. However, "common-sense knowledge" is all too often accepted as if it were "the gospel truth." The above summary specifically encourages research to test the statements of opinion in order to find out *whether or not* they are true. Some may think this to be a waste of time, energy, and money merely to verify what already is obvious, but it is important to recognize that many "obvious" relationships are supported by appeals to relatively few examples or even by the proverbial but false statement that "exceptions prove the rule." (Actually, they prove it to be false insofar as it is a statement of universality.)

Numerous common-sense beliefs have been proven false by careful research.

Since every kind of human reaction is conceivable, it is of great importance to know which reactions actually occur most frequently and under what conditions; only then will a more advanced social science develop.[10]

The sociologist studying evangelism will be very interested in the functional and dysfunctional consequences of various evangelistic structures, personnel, activities, and programs for the group which originates the evangelistic effort, for target individuals and groups, and for society as a whole. He will give attention to the evangelistic processes, appeals, and trends of various groups as well as to their goals and methods. He will be interested in analyzing the target audiences, the sources and backgrounds of new converts and of persons who refuse to be converted, the relationships between religious education and evangelism, the structural organizations concerned with evangelism, and the patterns of cooperation and antagonism between them.[11] Follow-up investigations to discover long-range effects on persons, institutions, and society will be an especially significant endeavor.[12]

Both the sociologist of religion, who is concerned with the "purely scientific" aspects of evangelism, and the applied sociologist, who serves religious groups as a researcher and consultant, can benefit from exploring the findings of research on other related subjects. For instance, studies of decision-making in business and personal life, of the adoption of new innovations in agriculture and education, of the communication process, of the effectiveness of the mass media of communications, of brainwashing and indoctrination in comparison to education and persuasion, of propaganda, of motivations, of group dynamics, and of a host of other topics can contribute many insights pertinent to religious behavior. These can be developed into hypotheses for testing by experimentation and other research methods.

Sociological research on evangelism must include consideration and study of the theological doctrines of various religious groups, of other church programs they sustain, of sectarian strife and conflict within and between churches as well as of cooperation among them, of social class and other sociological variables, and of a host of other topics. The reality behind some of these subjects may be unpleasant to acknowledge, but it is far better to face it realistically and to act rationally on the basis of facts than to attempt to wish unpleasing conditions away by pretending they do not exist. The exploitation of social science knowledge, theories, and research potentialities for the glory of God is a great need in contemporary Christendom.

Conclusion

There are many roadblocks to such uses of social science, however. Some of them are built into the professional positions and self-concepts of sociologists, while others arise from the ecclesiastical side.[13] One of the greatest problems is how to persuade clergy and laymen to use excellent resources which are already available and, even more significant, to apply their lessons.

Rather than discuss such matters here, let me indicate simply that most changes in evangelism are costly. They may save money, but they cost the time and effort of leaders who are compelled to change old traditions, to eradicate long-standing habits, to learn new methods, and to study the implications of these revisions and changes. They cost a commitment to service which imposes many demands upon those who serve. They cost the embarrassment of acknowledging weaknesses, errors, and failures that have been made in the past.

Research may reveal that the expanding toleration of all religious perspectives in our pluralistic society undercuts evangelism by subtly feeding the popular universalistic faith that any religion is equally good as long as one's beliefs, motives, and practices are sincere. It may even make it clear that only acceptance of a larger common core of faith based upon the New Testament can make it possible for the ecumenical movement to unite on the matter of evangelism.

When careful sociological research on evangelism has been done, I believe it will conclude that it is necessary to shift the site of evangelism from the church to the world of secular affairs, to acknowledge that the winds of change breathed by the Holy Spirit do not come solely through church hierarchies and the clergy, to minimize institutional goals for the sake of fulfilling the Christian mission more effectively, to admit openly through changed evangelistic practices that not all baptized church members are members of the Kingdom of God, and to insist upon a wholesome blending of evangelism and social concerns.

Notes

[1]It must be confessed, however, that many sociological hypotheses do not flow directly out of systematic social science theory; the discipline is still relatively underdeveloped, so it has not entirely reached that goal.

[2]David O. Moberg and Norris A. Magnuson, "Current Trends in Evangelism," *Journal of Pastoral Care,* Vol. X, No. 1 (Spring 1956), pp. 16-26 (quotation from p. 19).

[3]H. H. Gerth and C. Wright Mills, trans. and eds., *From Max Weber: Essays in Sociology* (New York: Oxford University Press, 1946), p. 280.

[4]*Ibid.*, pp. 280-281. Various Christian perspectives and biblical teachings on evangelism are summarized in Gordon R. Lewis, *Decide for Yourself: A Theological Workbook* (Downers Grove, Ill.: Inter-Varsity Press, 1970), pp. 143-148.

[5]See Martin Marty, *Varieties of Unbelief* (Garden City, N. Y.: Doubleday-Anchor Books, 1966).

[6]See Russell R. Dynes, "Church-Sect Typology and Socio-Economic Status," *American Sociological Review,* Vol. XX (October 1955), pp. 555-560, and Russell R. Dynes, "The Consequences of Sectarianism for Social Participation," *Social Forces,* Vol. XXXV (May 1957), pp. 331-334.

[7]David O. Moberg, "Does Social Class Shape the Church?" *Review of Religious Research,* Vol. I, No. 3 (Winter 1960), pp. 110-115.

[8]I do not mean to imply that no dysfunctional consequences result from religious competition. These also need to be identified and studied. Unfortunately, a balanced look at both the functions and dysfunctions is uncommon; those who are deeply committed to the ecumenical movement tend to see only one side, while its opponents keep their eyes open only to the other. The social scientist, qua scientist, aims to be objective, looking for all evidence pertinent to his hypotheses on both sides of this issue.

[9]Elihu Katz and Paul F. Lazarsfeld, *Personal Influence* (Glencoe, Ill.: The Free Press, 1955); Bernard R. Berelson, Paul F. Lazarsfeld, and William N. McPhee, *Voting* (Chicago: University of Chicago

Press, 1954); Paul F. Lazarsfeld, Bernard Berelson, and Hazel Gaudet, *The People's Choice* (New York: Columbia University Press, 2nd ed., 1948).

[10]Paul Lazarsfeld, "The American Soldier," *Public Opinion Quarterly,* Vol. XIII (Fall 1949), p. 380.

[11]See, for example, John A. Hostetler, *The Sociology of Mennonite Evangelism* (Scottdale, Pa.: Herald Press, 1954).

[12]For one such study see David O. Moberg and Norris A. Magnuson, "A Follow-up Study of Converts," *Bethel Seminary Quarterly,* Vol. III, No. 2, (February 1951), pp. 50-58.

[13]Although it omits direct consideration of applying sociology to organized religion, *Applied Sociology: Opportunities and Problems,* ed. by Alvin W. Gouldner and S. M. Miller (New York: The Free Press, 1965), is enlightening on many aspects of this problem.

Barriers to Effective Social Concern   5

Numerous polarities divide Christians today. Either-or thinking dominates many decisions; it drives some into one category of thought or action and others into the contrary position. When the differences coincide so that the same people consistently group together on one side and others on the opposite in a clear split, then these differences are destructive. But a multiplicity of conflicts also can knit a group together. If its cleavages involve different groupings of people on each specific issue of the divergent positions, then their differences help to solidify the larger group and to make it more lively and viable than it would be if everyone thought the same about every specific subject.[1]

Conflict about theological, philosophical, and practical issues therefore may serve either to divide a group into two or three warring camps or to unite it around central concerns into a web of criss-crossing interests in which individual members are sometimes working for and sometimes against the desires of other specific individuals. In other words, conflict sometimes supports the unity and solidarity of groups; it does not invariably break them down.

The division between people who think churches should stress evangelism and those who believe they should instead focus upon social action is related in fact, although not in logical necessity, to other forms of disjunctive (either-or) thinking and to several additional myths and errors about social problems and the nature and mission of the church. A few of these will be introduced in this chapter.

Neutrality

Social problems are extremely complex. Christians may be found on all sides of major policy issues. Many evangelicals therefore assume that the only truly Christian position is to abstain from all action by remaining "neutral," taking nobody's side in political controversy and concentrating instead on "saving souls."

Actually it is impossible not to take sides in a democratic society; neutrality supports the side of whoever wins in the struggle for power. Sometimes that side may be consistent with Christian values; more often it will support vested interests sustained by wealth, power, and privileged position. "Neutral" Christians thereby indirectly communicate that they believe those vested interests are morally right in social controversies.

Conformity with the world (Rom. 12:2) and participation in unfruitful works of darkness (Eph. 5:11) often result from unwittingly blessing the status quo by adopting a posture of alleged neutrality. In addition, direct literal statements of hundreds of Bible passages which state or imply that Christians must be actively concerned about social problems are implicitly denied by those who attempt to be neutral. They communicate the message to the world that the Christian gospel is totally irrelevant to practical contemporary problems except, perhaps, to provide comfort to their victims or possibly to change the motivations and aspirations of individual persons.

Churches and individuals who are unaware of the impossibility of neutrality and the inevitability of being involved with societal and "worldly" affairs tend to drift aimlessly with the ebb and flow of circumstances. They let themselves be conformed to the shape and tendencies of the present world age. Their refusal to take an active position constitutes a blessing upon the selfishness and covetousness which lie at the root of much political and economic life. No vote on positive efforts to bring about reforms in society constitutes a "No" vote; no vote on candidates for public office is the equivalent of casting a ballot for the winner, whoever he may be.[2] The aphorism, "All that is necessary for evil to triumph is for good men to do nothing," clearly applies to the question of alleged neutrality on political issues. To be neutral usually is to give one's support to evil.

Political inaction *is* action in a democracy. As Evangelist Tom Skinner said in his address to the American Baptist Convention in May 1971, the silence of "Bible-believing" Christians on social issues helps to sustain such lawbreakers as landlords whose apartments are rat-infested, rundown, and dilapidated; building code inspectors who are bribed by the landlords; those police whose presence in a black community constitutes a force only for maintaining the interests of white society; and public officials who "take poor people off subsidy and . . . put the Super Sonic Transport (SST) back on welfare again."[3]

Evangelical Christians have a tendency to react *against* political action more than to react *for* it. They are like the critics in Brickman's cartoon complaining about mistakes in the civil rights bill—"too weak, too little, too late, and too nothing." But their target of complaint replied, "Where were you when the pages were blank?"[4]

Louis Tamminga has pointed out that if Jael had let Sisera get away, he would have rebuilt his armies and attacked again in bitter fury (Judg. 4:12-22). Her doing nothing at all therefore would already have constituted an act against the people of God.[5] Thus it is today. Most of the time inaction is action against the will of God. It is impossible to be neutral.

Individualism

One of the greatest barriers to active social involvement is the belief that the basic causes of all social problems reside exclusively in individual persons, usually the victims. This is a strongly ingrained characteristic of American intellectual history, so it is not surprising that Christians conform to that perspective of their socio-cultural environment. Their biblical emphasis upon the importance of each individual's personal relationship with God accentuates an individualistic pattern of thinking about all issues which involve man.

Typical of this position is the statement of the Rev. Norman W. Berg at the third annual Lutheran Free Conference. He said that the mission of the church is the salvation of souls, not the redemption of society; the latter will be a "a natural by-product of the preaching of the gospel."[6] It is true that the "overflow of evangelical piety" stimulated numerous reforms in the nineteenth century, but as life became more complex, the individualism of frontier Protestantism began to serve as a means of ignoring and evading social problems. Success in evangelizing contributed to attitudes of exclusivism which hampered effective action to meet the challenges of the new day. This Great Reversal exemplifies Arnold Toynbee's "idolization of the ephemeral."[7]

American revivalism ever since the days of Finney has emphasized an individualistic approach in which sin is reduced to simple, personal proportions and the solution to it similarly is very personal—the regeneration of in-

dividual souls. The essence of the pietism which revivalists extol is alleged ultimately to have "contributed more
toward making men conform than reform," thus contributing to making America one of the most materialistic
and secularistic nations in the world.[8] The language of
individualistic piety easily "degenerates into a smug and
nagging moralism."[9]

Most white Americans simultaneously reject racist beliefs and accept the racist perspective that those black
individuals who really want to get ahead can do so. By
thus espousing the simplistic individualistic position that
the race problem is simply one of the free will of its
victims, they deny the reality of the problems of discrimination confronted by black Americans and naively
place the entire burden of racial disadvantages on the
minority group. They have not experienced, as blacks
have, the heavy oppression of public and private institutions, values, and actions which limit opportunities and
prevent them from receiving equal rewards for their
efforts. "Most of all, white Americans do not understand
that individual free will operates and has its beneficial
effects only within institutional contexts that give it
efficacy and purpose."[10]

In similar manner, the problems of substandard housing for the poor are frequently attributed to the owners of
such housing "because they are evil men." Nevertheless,
there are hundreds of thousands of such landlords, many
of whom are making such small profits that under-
maintenance of the property is both a rational and necessary means of survival. They enjoy a symbiotic relationship with their tenants, each needing the other and
providing for the other something they need.

The owners need the poor and troubled because few others
would consider living in depressed housing; and who but the

poor and troubled must seek the cheapest possible shelter? . . .
The notion that owners of substandard units cause the sickness
and suffering that plague the unfortunate families who dwell
there sounds suspiciously like an inversion of the "good housing—good people" theory.[11]

Thus with one social problem after another it can be
demonstrated that the causes, implications, consequences, effects, and interrelationships demand treatment
on a grand social-systems level in order to be effective in
our complex society. Changing the hearts and minds of
individual persons is by itself inadequate; the entire
social system needs radical change at numerous points, as
we shall see in Chapter 7.

Despite this societal need, the most distinctive and
obvious trait Hadden found in his national survey of
college seniors was *privatism,* the withdrawal from institutions into the self. The students were idealistic and
socially aware, contemptuous of the older generation's
hypocrisy in failing to break out of institutional restraints
to act upon stated ideals, lacking in a realistic sense of
what their ideals imply in terms of social and public
action, ambiguous in the implications of their privatism
ethic, which tended to be self-centered and anti-
institutional, and assuming a high level of materialistic
comfort which seemed unbridled by any social norm or
tradition. They lacked an integrated value system, were
docilely conformed to the stated ideals of parents and
teachers, rejected authority, and desired to follow their
own modes of conduct. Their privatism ethic tended to
turn into a kind of romantic withdrawal, an escape from
responsibility to others and society into a totally personal
world.[12]

The individualistic, privatistic ethic is not limited,
however, to youth.[13] It is very widespread throughout our

culture. It is an opponent to all concern for others, including both the evangelistic and social-action varieties. Hear, for example, the message of Bill Barnes, "a prophetic man in the American wilderness," who is minister at Edgehill Methodist Church in a black district of Nashville. He suggests that one of the factors hindering the change that is fostered by black religious self-consciousness, the youth culture, urbanization, and secularization is the increasing suburbanization of American society which works

. . . to keep churches privatized and "spiritual." People move to suburbs, so obviously do churches. The dizzy mobility of American families in suburbs practically demands that churches serve (and stick to) a socializing, a familizing, a stabilizing function. Anything else is unwanted, unneeded, resented. The world of daily work, of urban politics, or racial tensions, or stark poverty is miles away at the other end of the commuter route. And this is true by choice and determination. Not a very likely set of social forces in which to generate social change![14]

Social Darwinism

Individualism is linked very readily with but slightly modernized forms of the Social Darwinism that played such a strong role in sanctioning the activities of the "robber barons," "warlords of capitalism," and other business magnates of England and the United States during the latter part of the nineteenth century. It taught that the fittest survive, so it provided a rationalization for their position of wealth and privilege and endorsed the greedy grasping after ever more wealth and power. Those who managed to survive the competitive struggle and rose to the top, even if through ruthless cutthroat competition, "obviously" were the fittest.

The evolution of society was assumed by Social Darwinists to occur the most rapidly and surely when complete freedom prevails without any restrictive barriers imposed by government. They believed that when government introduces special projects to help people as individuals or as members of organizations, it hinders the process of survival of the fittest, enabling many unfit to survive. There ought to be no public programs of harbor improvement, for they would help unfit pilots find their way to port. There should be no programs of vaccination, for they would prevent many unfit from dying and thus would permit them to propagate another generation of their own unfit kind. Similarly schools, postal systems, social welfare, hospitals, highways, and almost everything except military defense should be left in the hands of private competitive business. Only thus could the process of natural selection operate to weed out unfit persons and unfit organizations.[15]

Contemporary right-wing extremists have a practical program to implement their ideals which is almost identical to that of the Social Darwinists of the 1880's and 1890's. Christians among them present their programs and objectives under the guise of Bible proof-texts and high-sounding moral norms,[16] but the practical effects of their programs are no less dubious than those of their philosophical forebears a century ago.

Past and present Social Darwinists have failed to recognize many things. For example, winning positions of wealth and power generally was a result of control over certain natural resources or of the ability to use the labor of others. It was not a consequence solely of personal qualifications and efforts. The adverse social and economic positions of most deprived people have resulted more from environmental than from hereditary influences. Personal characteristics considered desirable vary greatly with time, place, and circumstances, so the very ones being eliminated in one era may be highly desirable in another. The traits of any person are so numerous that each has a complex commingling of both desirable and undesirable features, whether he is among "successes" or "failures."

Those who accept the Social Darwinist philosophy of free and unfettered competition as the basis for the evolution or progress of society tend also to oppose any kind of governmental action to deal with the problems of mankind. When their perspectives are linked with words associated with Christianity or proof-texts from the Bible, they accentuate individualism and sanction the refusal to accept the social ethics which are an essential part of truly Christian faith.

Conservatism-Liberalism

One of the most significant conflicts among Christians today relates to the polarization of "conservatives" and "liberals" which is occurring within all major denominational bodies. Aubrey B. Haines believes that this rift threatens their ability to fulfill their functions, for the liberals have a this-worldly orientation that tends to confine Christianity to a "works theology," while the conservatives have an otherworldly orientation that confines it to a "faith theology," and neither recognizes that faith and works cannot be separated.[17]

In their drive for consistency Christians tend to slip into the trap of assuming that liberalism or conservatism constitutes a single, unitary orientation toward life, the universe, and God. Some of the most respected spokesmen of evangelicalism work diligently to promote and strengthen the linkage between theological and socioeconomic-political conservatism. They teach, preach, and reinforce the perspective that all who are orthodox in their Christian faith must be conservative in every other respect. As a result, their followers assume that there is a specific and clear Christian position on current issues; they are taught that evangelicals "obviously" should favor defense of states' rights in contrast to expansion of the federal domain, oppose government taxation of the middle and upper classes for the purpose of public welfare programs to help the poor, support the American Way of Life as "God's ideal" for all people everywhere, oppose the United Nations as leading toward loss of national autonomy and ultimate enthronement of the great 666 Ruler of Rev. 13:18, uphold laissez-faire capi-ialism as the only "Christian" economic system, defend the use of capital punishment, support the military-industrial position with regard to war, and accept other specific stands as "the" Christian position.

When intelligent and socially sensitive youths see that "the" evangelical position on political, economic, and social affairs corresponds closely to that of the wealthy and powerful vested interests in society, that it is in many cases detrimental to the best interests of ethnic and cultural minorities and other deprived people, that it is inconsistent with many facts of the social and behavioral sciences, that it is incompatible with Christian values, and that their elders refuse to reconsider their stubbornly conservative positions, they tend to drop out of evangelical churches and join movements which protest against the hypocrisies of "the establishment."

Concern for evangelism must be broad enough to include concern for these youthful and adult defections from the churches. We do not know how much of the "de-evangelization" occurring by members who drop out of their congregations is directly linked with either too much or too little social alertness and concern. Certainly research is needed on this subject to test the contrasting hypotheses of various opinion leaders.

Social, economic, and political conservatism among Christians often encourages them to be uninvolved in political life, except to oppose most efforts to bring about social change which do not represent something other than going "back to the good old days." Boundary-maintenance efforts to remain distinct from theological liberals who work for progressive changes and the human tendency to link together into one lump everything one hates are parts of the causal background for this tendency. Other causes are fear of the unknown, a desire to "play it safe," the pessimistic outlook that change invariably and inevitably must be for the worse rather than the better, the desire not to alienate Grandpa Jones whose faithful support of the church indicates he may leave it a substantial legacy if he is not alienated by political views contrary to his own, the belief that we should remain separate from the world, the feeling that eternal values are represented only by the personal salvation of souls, the anti-intellectualism of many evangelical leaders which denounces "human wisdom," the relatively narrow group identifications and social contacts of many evangelicals, their rural orientation and backgrounds, the publications that are popularly read by them which are predominantly on the conservative end of the sociopolitical spectrum, and other social and intellectual influences.

The crystallization of attitudes is strongest among persons who have few social pressures. In other words, the narrower the social contacts and affiliations of an individual, the greater the degree to which his attitudes are either consistently liberal or consistently conservative.[18] Dogmatic views held in ignorance will dissipate only when eyes are opened to the previously unnoticed true nature of human needs. Exposure to others helps to reveal people and problems that call for the healing touch of the gospel.

A major cause of conservatism among evangelicals is conformity with the world. Efforts by Christians to resist changes in basic social institutions and the equating of Americanism with Christianity both imply that present social structures are viewed as either God's best for man or else as so totally unredeemable that any change is worse than no change. Calvin Redekop believes that the greatest peril for Christians is "the trap of cultural seduction."[19] Certainly Christians are warned sharply and clearly against the sin of being conformed to the world system of this age (Rom. 12:2). This means, among other things, that they cannot be either doctrinaire liberals or dyed-in-the-wool conservatives. To put socioeconomic or political loyalties first and Christian values second is a form of idolatry, a type of elevating a false god to the position of God Almighty.

Neither conservatism nor liberalism is a unitary concept. All possible combinations of political, economic, religious, social, and esthetic liberalism-conservatism may be found even in relatively small groups.[20] People may be liberal with respect to their beliefs about a guaranteed annual wage, conservative about the need for "law and order," and middle-of-the-road in their attitudes toward the United Nations, to mention only three political components of the liberalism-conservatism bundle of issues. Again, one may be highly conservative in his belief that Jesus Christ was bodily resurrected from His grave but very liberal in his perspectives about the structural forms and program of His church. Peter J. Henriot's research on this complex subject led him to the conclusion that we must "beware of the easy assumption that 'a liberal is a liberal is a liberal.'"[21]

Many theological liberals are ultra-conservative on social, political, and economic issues, and many theological conservatives are socioeconomically liberal. We must avoid "the unequal yoke" that ties evangelical Christianity tightly and unquestioningly to the societal status quo in the false assumption that being conservative in one area necessitates conservatism in the other.[22]

It is likely that the majority of even the most reactionary conservatives have at least some liberal perspectives. They may have modernistic and liberal tastes, for example, when purchasing an automobile, planning to build or remodel a home, buying clothes, or having their hair styled. Politically they are likely to be liberal whenever such a position will benefit themselves. Recognition of this fact should help to overcome the unjustifiable equation of evangelicalism with either socioeconomic and political conservatism which hinders an effective social concern or with the liberalism that presumes a specific "Christian" response in advance of any investigation.

Other Impediments

A large number of additional problems hamper effective Christian action relevant to social issues. Only a brief summary of a few of them is possible here.

It is often felt—perhaps largely because of the individualism rampant in both the American culture and its churches—that Christian love can be extended only on a personal level. This attitude is reflected in an aloofness toward direct involvement in collective approaches to the prevention, treatment, alleviation, and solution of social problems. Such people do not realize that *all social problems are intensely personal to the individuals who are their victims* and that work on the mass level of societal action can help thousands of people at once, while aiding victims is typically on only a one-to-one basis.[23]

Misinformation and lack of understanding of the complex causes, effects, and solutions of social problems are another source of difficulty.[24] It is very tempting to attribute all problems to sin, and indeed it is true that, theologically speaking, sin is the ultimate source. It is not always the sin of the victims, however, that produces their sorry plight, nor do upright Christians escape being victimized by social problems. Furthermore, conversion does not automatically rescue people out of misery; words of peace do not take the place of food and clothing (James 2:14-17). The righteous man today is tempted as of old to wonder why so many wicked people prosper, while many righteous do not (Pss. 73 and 94). It is easy to say, "Sin is the cause," and "Jesus is the answer." But the immediate specific applications of such beliefs are so vague, and their implications are so complex, that little practical guidance results from expressing such shibboleths. The complex issue of relationships between evangelism and social concern is but one of the numerous facets of the question of *how* Jesus Christ can be or become the answer to sin and human social needs.

We have already mentioned the temptation to become imbalanced by either emphasizing the words of the gospel to the exclusion of deeds of social concern or trying to be the love of God, demonstrating it without any words of proclamation at all. Either position is heresy. (This is not intended to deny that the functional specialization of Christians may make it appropriate for some to emphasize one form of witness while others stress another, all reinforcing and supporting each other in a web of

Christian influence and action.) Both the verbal message and the social services are needed!

The criticisms of youth about the hypocrisy lodged in churches sometimes compel people to withdraw unwisely from efforts to deal with human needs. They are led to the false conclusion that unless one is completely right with God, he cannot serve others. Since no one can live a life of perfect personal piety and impeccable social relationships on this side of the grave, this perspective results in a complete withdrawal of service. In humility the relatively mature Christian realizes that he is still growing toward perfection; he may make grievous errors, but this does not deter him from pursuing the righteousness of Christ in regard to both personal piety and social action. Similarly, he recognizes that his motives are always tainted, so he must not wait to do good until they are perfectly pure; that day will not arrive in the present life.[25] If Christians would acknowledge their imperfections more often, pose as perfected saints less often, and proclaim more clearly that they still are sinners and their righteousness is imputed from Christ, fewer charges of hypocrisy would be leveled against them.

Among the common fallacies about the role of Christians and the church in dealing with social problems are these erroneous beliefs:

—that good intentions are a sufficient basis for social action and in themselves constitute service.

—that love is strictly an attitude and does not demand anything more than a mental orientation.[26]

—that the act of passing resolutions about problems meets the entire need for concerted church action.[27]

—that spiritual virtues qualify people for precise details of political action (the fallacy of misplaced expertise).[28]

—that "pure preaching" of justification by faith or devotion to Christ without specific applications will automatically lead to correct Christian action.[29]

—that loving sinners by helping to provide some of their material needs is equivalent to condoning their sins or approving their sinfulness.

—that failure must be avoided at all costs, so innovative action with uncertain results or high risk should be shunned.

—that one can love human "souls" without being concerned for their bodies.

—that it is possible for dedicated Christians to be devoted to fulfilling intense spiritual concerns without also being concerned about the social, physical, and material needs of men.

—that all distinctively American values are Christian values which every nation should adopt.

—that a decision to act is the same as the action itself.

—that Christian witnessing pertains only to words—or only to deeds—instead of to the totality of what a Christian is and does.

—that it is possible to find solutions to social evil without the costs of sacrificing taxes, time, prestige, pride, reputation, traditions, and self-denial.

—that the "secular" can be separated legitimately from the "sacred" realm of life.

—that Christian faith pertains only to the sacred.

All of these affect Christians' attempts to meet their obligations to evangelize and to exercise Christian social concern.

The polarities that divide Christians into contrasting ideological categories reflect the Great Reversal. To a considerable extent they are a result of the failure to understand adequately both what the Bible teaches and the principles and knowledge about society and man revealed by the social and behavioral sciences. Erroneous and incomplete knowledge on both levels helps to promote heretical thought, perpetuate injustice, accentuate worldliness, strengthen the forces of evil in society, hamper Christ-honoring changes, hinder the conversion of sinners, and deny the fact that Christians are pilgrims who cannot be anchored absolutely to any earthly system.

Notes

[1]Lewis A. Coser, *The Functions of Social Conflict* (Glencoe, Ill.: The Free Press, 1956), esp. pp. 78-80.

[2]See related discussions in David O. Moberg, *Inasmuch: Christian Social Responsibility in the Twentieth Century* (Grand Rapids, Mich.: Eerdmans, 1965), pp. 14-16, 21, 113.

[3]"U. S. Needs Black for President in 1972, Baptist Convention Told," *Minneapolis Star*, May 15, 1971, p. 9-A.

[4]Brickman, "The Small Society," *St. Paul Dispatch,* August 22, 1966, p. 11 (Washington Star Syndicate, Inc.).

[5]Louis Tamminga, "Great Searchings of Heart," *The Guide* (Christian Labour Association of Canada), Vol. XIX, No. 7-9 (Labour Day, 1971), pp. 10-11.

[6]"Church's Role Spiritual, Not Social, Free Conference Told," *The Lutheran Layman,* Vol. XXXVII, No. 8 (August 1966), p. 6.

[7]Quoted in Will Herberg, *Protestant—Catholic—Jew* (Garden City, N. Y.: Doubleday-Anchor Books, rev. ed., 1960), pp. 116-117.

[8]William G. McLoughlin, Jr., *Modern Revivalism: Charles Grandison Finney to Billy Graham* (New York: Ronald Press, 1959), p. 527. (The opposite fallacy of stressing social reform without any concern for personal piety is equally dangerous.)

[9]Herberg, *op. cit.,* p. 120.

[10]Howard Schuman, "Sociological Racism," *Trans-Action,* Vol. VII, No. 2 (December 1969), pp. 44-48 (quotation from p. 48).

[11]Michael A. Stegman, "The New Mythology of Housing," *Trans-Action,* Vol. VII, No. 3 (January 1970), pp. 55-62 (quotation from p. 57).

[12]Jeffrey K. Hadden, "The Private Generation," *Psychology Today,* Vol. III, No. 5 (October 1969), pp. 32-35, 68-69.

[13]Roger Mehl in *The Sociology of Protestantism,* James H. Farley, trans. (Philadelphia: Westminister Press, 1970) states that secularization is one of its sources, for it causes churches to withdraw to a differentiat-

ed, specialized role of performing "purely spiritual tasks," which sociologically are private (p. 276).

[14]Bill Barnes, "The Church in the Seventies," *Vanderbilt Divinity Review,* Winter 1971, pp. 14-19 (quotation from p. 17).

[15]Several works of William Graham Sumner and Herbert Spencer, the leading theorists of Social Darwinism, have been reprinted in recent years. One of the best scholarly discussions of its past history is Richard Hofstadter, *Social Darwinism in American Thought, 1860-1915* (Philadelphia: University of Pennsylvania Press, 1945). See also Charles G. Cleaver, "Traces of Social Darwinism in Contemporary America," *The Christian Scholar,* Vol. XLIV, No. 4 (Winter 1961), pp. 332-342. For current examples of Social Darwinist literature (although it does not use that label) see *The Freeman* and *Human Events.*

[16]"Christian economics" is a prominent example.

[17]Aubrey B. Haines, "Polarization within the Churches," *Christian Century,* Vol. LXXXVII, No. 35 (September 2, 1970), pp. 1039-1041.

[18]Marvin E. Olsen, "Liberal-Conservative Attitude Crystallization," *Sociological Quarterly,* Vol. III, No. 1 (January 1962), pp. 17-26.

[19]Calvin Redekop, *The Free Church and Seductive Culture* (Scottdale, Pa.: Herald Press, 1971).

[20]Willard A. Kerr, "Untangling the Liberalism-Conservatism Continuum," *Journal of Social Psychology,* Vol. XXXV (February 1952), pp. 111-125.

[21]Peter J. Henriot, S. J., "The Coincidence of Political and Religious Attitudes," *Review of Religious Research,* Vol. VIII (Fall 1966), p. 57.

[22]Richard V. Pierard, *The Unequal Yoke* (Philadelphia: J. B. Lippincott, 1970).

[23]See Moberg, *op. cit.,* pp. 62-64.

[24]*Ibid.,* pp. 61-78. See also any of the numerous current college textbooks on the subject of Social Problems.

[25]*Ibid.,* pp. 41-43.

[26]*Ibid.,* pp. 43-44.

[27]*Ibid.,* pp. 124-126.

[28]See Paul Ramsey, *Who Speaks for the Church?* (Nashville: Abingdon Press, 1967).

[29]Research has shown that this "theological romanticism" is common among ministers. See, e.g., Henry Clark, *The Church and Residential Desegregation* (New Haven, Conn.: College and University Press, 1965), esp. p. 193.

Social Welfare and Evangelism

As we have seen, the relationship between evangelism and social welfare is a current issue among Christians of most, if not all, denominations. It temporarily subsided but did not become passé with the gradual decline of the fundamentalist-modernist controversies in which evangelistically oriented Christians were arrayed against social gospelites on numerous issues. Its implications lie at the heart of many contemporary problems of church-state relationships and religious liberty. It is one of the important topics demanding exploration in attempts to develop a consistent Protestant philosophy of social concern. Today, as in 1936 and 1955, there are numerous orientations of social welfare within the Protestant heritage but "no generally accepted philosophy of social work under religious auspices, or of relationships to community agencies and public welfare services."[1]

At times it seems as if discussions of relationships between evangelism and social welfare are shunned by religious leaders, but lay Christians are seeking satisfying answers. One of the key issues of special pertinence to evangelicals is the extent to which and the manner in which governmentally subsidized social welfare programs are used as instruments of evangelism. If social welfare is a tool in the evangelistic work of the church, and if that welfare is supported by public funds, then governmental resources are being used to promote Christian or sectarian evangelism. (The term *evangelism* is interpreted here as including the total task of promulgating the gospel in order to win converts to one's faith. As we saw in Chapter 4, it has a wide range of specific meanings as well as of theological interpretations and practical techniques among contemporary Christians.)

Social welfare refers to all the social services that are provided by social workers, medical doctors, clinical psychologists, counselors, and people in other relevant helping professions, together with their paraprofessional and volunteer helpers. Its primary orientation is toward the victims of social problems, in contrast to *social action,* which aims to correct the social structures and processes of society that cause the problems. Social welfare covers a very wide range of agencies and activities, including retirement homes, institutional care of children, child placement and adoption, community centers, neighborhood houses, family welfare agencies, sheltered workshops, rehabilitation centers, halfway houses, emergency clinics, and similar facilities. For most purposes, convalescent homes, health clinics, drug treatment centers, hospitals, chaplaincy services, camping programs, recreational services, and institutional educational programs also can be treated as aspects of social welfare. Evangelism often motivates social welfare.

Characteristics of Motives

It is difficult to specify precisely what is meant by motives. In everyday usage they are the incentives, inducements, enticements, goals, needs, and reasons that move a person to action. We tend to see them as linked closely with the human will when we think them to be conscious influencers of behavior, but we use them to explain otherwise inexplicable behavior as if they are totally irrational products of feeling, emotion, and the unconscious when we fail to identify the conscious operation of specific drives, desires, or dispositions which we presume to be the internal cause of a person's actions.

Some psychologists believe that the concept of motivation should be repudiated entirely because it is a verbal reification that clutters up our understanding of man.[2] Rather than quibble about definitions, let us take it for granted that our use of the concept is basically in accord with everyday meanings of the term but centers upon "the consciously avowed objectives which provide direction, unity, and organization to a succession of movements."[3]

Motives are extremely complex. The "reasons why" we engage in any volitional act are numerous. When challenged to give an explanation of a deed, we may reply in terms of predisposing habits, past experiences, precipitating events, predictions from background knowledge, expectations inherent in our definition of the situation, communication channels that stimulated our responses, rationalizations of our reference group, alternatives among which the choice was made, verbal stereotypes conventionally labeled as "motives," internal stimuli known as drives, categorical responses that assume the act was automatic or natural or the only proper way of behaving, value judgments of moral standards, or even a mere description of the situation.

There is seldom, if ever, but one motive for any voluntary act. The motives are not only numerous; they are also diffused, difficult to identify, and tightly intermingled with one another. The isolation of any one motive is a task for interpretative analysis, for motives cannot be seen empirically like objects outside the mind of man. Man is a whole being. His multiple and mixed motives cannot be severed from him in the same manner as a finger, hair, or toenail.

When one tries to identify his motives for an act, he may arrive at quite different conclusions from those of another person who is analyzing or diagnosing the same behavior. In religious contexts, as in others, we tend to attribute lofty motives to the behavior of ourselves and our reference groups but corrupt motives to the behavior of those who are in competition or conflict with us. Among Protestants there has been a definite tendency to accuse Catholics of ulterior motives like proselytism, gaining the advantages of political power, or increasing institutional strength through certain programs, but their own comparable activities are alleged to be for the sake of the Kingdom of God or are seen as purely altruistic acts of love with no thought of self-gain!

When the motives of a person are so complex, it is folly to try to identify all the motives involved in an institutional program of social welfare which has broad and diverse activities with dozens or even thousands of individuals playing their multifarious roles in numerous times and places. Nevertheless, we can attempt to abstract selected elements of this complex reality for purposes of our discussion, recognizing that the motives of sponsoring agencies, contributors, administrators, caseworkers, other personnel, and recipients are all part of the total picture from which this oversimplified version comes.

Social Welfare as Evangelistic Bait

Historically many Christian groups have used charity and welfare programs as a means of evangelism.

In the early days of religious social work, there was seldom any question but that the church-sponsored worker who dealt with human need also ministered to souls. The visiting nurse closed her visits with prayer. . . . The church visitor dispensing relief also attempted to convert unbelievers. . . . [There was a] complete integration of the evangelical and welfare motivations. . . . [4]

A closely related motive is reflected in child adoption programs which, in their appeals for financial support, for babies, and for adopting parents, emphasize the idea that Protestant child adoption services prevent babies from being reared as Catholics, help more children grow up in Protestant homes, and thus contribute to the relative strength of Protestantism or even of a specific denomination.

Evangelistic motivations are very strong in social welfare programs for American Indians, Puerto Ricans, Cubans, and other minority ethnic groups as well as in church programs for migrant workers and in gospel missions. For example, a Southern Baptist brochure includes these statements:

The rescue mission is a soul-saving place, a place where human wreckage is salvaged through the making over of lives by the gospel's power. . . . By the grace of God it is able not only to put a new suit on a man, but, even more important, to put a new man in the suit.

The mission is a place devoted to the regenerating, reconditioning, rehabilitating of human derelicts who have been wrecked by the storms of life. The mission is a spiritual awakener and a crime preventer. It is a soul-saving institution.[5]

A significant doctrinal paper for the Lutheran Church—Missouri Synod includes these statements:

The Scriptures teach that welfare work, when carried on by the Church, should not be an end in itself, as it is with the State, but an activity whereby the doer exercises his faith and the recipient is brought into contact with the Gospel, which alone is the means by which the Holy Ghost begets spiritual life.

. . . Christian welfare aims at bringing the recipient into

contact with the Gospel, either to beget faith in him, or, if he is already a child of God, to strengthen him in his faith. . . . the ultimate end of Christian welfare work is to do good to the soul of man.[6]

Foreign missions programs which include social welfare activities have openly used them as "bait" in their work of "fishing for men." Sometimes the recipients of these services have become disillusioned with Christianity when they have gained the not unwarranted impression that deeds which at first appeared to involve love were performed as a means to the end of winning converts for the benefit of the missionaries. At home as well as abroad, Christians have engaged in acts of giving to which hidden price tags have been attached. In order to receive a bowl of soup or a bed for the night, the rescue-mission client must listen to a sermon. To continue receiving material assistance, poverty-stricken families may be required by subtle, unspoken rules to express their thanks publicly. A tract may accompany a check, or assistance may be linked with instruction. Unless the givers are rewarded with ego-inflating praise, the recipients may be considered unworthy and might be cut off from future help. Negative results of such evangelism include pride by the donor because of his superior status, his assumption that others are in greater need of repentance, dedication, or religious education than himself, and even "the heresy that equates worldly success with grace."[7]

The expansion of professional social work, as well as the detrimental results for both the givers and recipients from welfare that has strings of ulterior motives attached, has led to a renunciation of the evangelistic motive by most church-related welfare agencies. In striving to attain and maintain high professional status religion in any form except the most generalized of naturalistic and humanistic tenets has tended to be excluded from the church related agencies. . . .

Along with the disappearance of overt religious content has gone much of the moral exhortation that characterized earlier welfare work under religious auspices. . . .[8]

When formal religious activities are permitted in homes for the aged, children's institutions, neighborhood houses, hospitals, and other agencies, they have become increasingly isolated and segregated. In the effort not to force religious faith on anyone, religious programs have become specialized services performed by professional chaplains, limited to chapel services, or confined to pastoral counseling for those who request it. Meanwhile, however, reports to the sponsoring religious body tend to play up any successful religious activity, such as persons received into church membership or new Sunday school pupils gained through the welfare agency. When this is a basic motive and it is not forthrightly acknowledged, questions about honesty can be raised. Similarly, when Protestants justify their support of social services which are no different from public or private "secular" programs by declaring them to be "a public witness to the nature of Christian faith," is there any true witness at all if the service is not identified as specifically Christian by recipients or others in the community?[9]

In addition, however, it must be remembered that in our pluralistic society the client who has a choice of social agencies to meet his particular needs may choose a sectarian agency specifically because of its religious auspices. He may be seeking help within a known and desired context of religious beliefs and practices in a conscious or unconscious hope that spiritual ministries will accompany the other social welfare services.[10]

The very fact of church sponsorship of agencies and institutions providing compassionate and competent services often gives these services the character of preparation for, or expression of, the gospel, which would not be nearly so likely in a different setting.[11]

Welfare Is Witness

Rather than using social welfare as either a type of bait or as a hook to catch converts, the majority of church-related social work agencies today may be seen as basically centers of service rather than of verbal proclamation. Welfare is interpreted as an expression and result of the gospel which at the same time is a witness to it. "Church-related agencies constitute one of the visible means by which the Lord's compassion is expressed in the world today."[12] Accepting the sinner as he is and showering love upon him through welfare communicates the love of God.

In its *Resource Book for Evangelism,* the Commission on Evangelism of the Lutheran Church in America includes Christian social ministry in the community as an aspect of "the larger evangelism." However, it does not see this in terms of old-fashioned buttonholing and revivalistic pressure techniques.

Christian action to minister to whatever sickness or sorrow exists, as well as to meet the social needs of the time, testifies to the reality of the love of God. Frequent expressions of loving concern both among members and toward non-members are part of that total ministry through which the congregation proclaims the gospel. . . . Through all of [these services] the congregation is both providing a social ministry and bearing witness. It is communicating Christ's love in deeds as well as words.[13]

Just as the words of Jesus are inseparable from His works, both being eloquent witnesses of His ministry, so witnessing today occurs by deeds as well as by words. Worship without witnessing and active concern for the welfare of others tends to become dead form. Witnessing without worship and welfare tends to create a "church of words" instead of a Church of the Word. Welfare without worship and witness may change the church into merely a social agency; all three of these "w's of life" are needed, and all are inseparably bound together in the Christian church.[14] Indeed, welfare work which continues in the footsteps of the Lord's assistance to the needy and ministry of healing may be seen as "a token of man's total redemption when our Lord returns in royal splendor."[15]

Some have referred to Christian social service as "the new evangelism." We live in an age which is increasingly aware of nonverbal communication—the "silent language" of behavior[16]—and of the hypocrisy that becomes evident when actions do not correspond to verbal messages. Christians are under as great pressures as ever before, if not greater, to live as well as to speak the gospel. This-worldly testimony of deeds is expected to balance otherworldly aspirations. Social welfare and an active participation in social action for the benefit of mankind help to proclaim the good news of God's love to the world. As an Anglican clergyman put it:

> . . . it may well be that social service performed by those whose motivation is clearly Christian will prove to be the most effective and compelling evangelism. . . .
> . . . Christian social service is not an end in itself—it is a means to an end. The end is . . . wholeness, salvation. . . . Christian social service is a means, a means by which men may be helped to re-enter that loving relationship with God and his fellows which fallen man has lost. . . . Such salvation is accomplished by one means and only one and that is by redemptive love, not by social manipulation.[17]

Evangelism and Social Welfare

Evangelism may be considered a motive behind social welfare in another respect. By introducing the love of God into the heart of man, it becomes a motivating force that compels Christians to establish welfare services.

Fundamentalists are inclined to stress this strongly, sometimes so strongly that others suspect their motives. Many of them hold that the evils of this world are a result of personal sins. Only by converting men to Christ can these evils be overcome, so collective social action is shunned in favor of what they call "genuine spiritual motivations" flowing out of an inner, Christ-like love to individuals who are in need. Unfortunately, their goal of seeing all men converted is unrealistic in this present age. In addition, not all who make "decisions for Christ" are fully converted in all of their behavior to the Christian way of life; indeed all remain sinners saved by grace. "If we say we have no sin, we deceive ourselves, and the truth is not in us" (I John 1:8). Christian nurture is necessary to develop the motivation to love and to reveal its practical implications for conduct.

Statements by denominational leaders on the motiva tion for Christian welfare work most often emphasize the love, example, and teachings of Christ. The needs of men, the ethical teachings of the New Testament, regard for man's dignity and worth, moral responsibility or duty, a passion for justice, evangelism, and missionary goals are among the other diverse motives listed.[18] To a degree, at least, all these may be seen as products of evangelism or conversion.

Social work and evangelism share many similar orientations and motives. Both focus upon needs of the person who is the object of their endeavors, whether he correctly identifies his needs or not. Both believe that he can be helped. Both are motivated by the hope that the recipient will respond and change. In both the response involves a voluntary choice. Both, at least when at their best, recognize the interrelatedness and interdependence of all men. Both recognize the uniqueness of each person and yet the existence of common human needs. Both are concerned with preventing problems in the future and with alleviating the impact of those which already have emerged.[19]

Nevertheless, social work is not evangelism, and vice versa. They represent different tasks in the division of labor of the body of Christ. Their goals differ in several respects. The evangelistic goal "is, primarily, to bring the individual to a knowledge of God; that of the social worker is to help the individual make an adjustment to society."[20] What the social worker interprets as a symptom, the minister may label "sin." The caseworker operates outside of a formal recognition of God's presence in his relationship with a person in trouble, and an adequate adjustment within himself and to society does not necessarily require any religious conviction or church activity. Many ministers see social agencies only as "a court of last resort when all has failed, or as a mother of necessity when social work seems to control the administration of special functions such as public relief, admission to institutions, etc."[21] Tensions between the professions result from these differences. When evangelistically inclined ministers control social agencies, they find it extremely difficult to secure and hold professional social workers on the staff.

In church-related agencies it is possible, however, to develop a person-centered program which makes religious resources a normal part of available services.

Social Welfare and Evangelism

Concern for the welfare of the whole man certainly implies a need to give attention to spiritual as well as material, psychological, physical, and social needs. This necessitates bringing social welfare and evangelism together (along with worship, education, and social fellowship) in mutually enriching fruitful relationships.

Separation of Church and State

If Christian ideals are upheld in action as well as in affirmation, Christians in social work and other helping professions will strive persistently to fulfill their mission as laymen who are witnesses to Jesus Christ twenty-four hours of every day. This means that an implicit evangelistic dimension will be a part of their vocation whether they work in public, secular, or church-related agencies. Whenever we deliberately encourage Christians to enter such key occupations as school teaching, politics, medicine, social work, and the various other helping professions as part of the thrust to extend the Kingdom of God, we are encouraging the perspective that no worthy role in life is "secular," for all can be sanctified to the praise of God. Such "Christian infiltration" into positions paid by or subsidized with governmental funds is generally given our blessing. Does this imply that, in order to be consistent, we ought to encourage the expansion of government subsidies for church-related welfare?

Of 986 denominationally known health and welfare agencies and institutions surveyed in 1955, eighty-seven percent stated that they had a religious objective; ninety-six percent considered themselves Christian in tradition, spirit, motivation of personnel, and the like, and about two-thirds provided distinctly religious services.[22]

Religious services and activities are not limited to church-related agencies, however. An increasing proportion of public institutions and programs provide chaplains, worship services, religious education, and other activities that include, at the least, the possibility of evangelistic work. There also is a growing concern in professional social work for "inner space," which includes a spiritual dimension, and the drive for dealing with man's "wholeness" is leading some social workers into an active consideration of the positive values that can come through the use of religious resources.[23]

In response to this trend, will we as evangelicals, out of our traditional stance pertinent to religious liberty and the separation of church and state, insist that religious perspectives must be omitted entirely from public welfare resources? If we insist that no governmental funds whatever be used for any type of welfare services which are provided for church-related agencies, we ought also to insist that no religious perspectives and resources—including those of evangelicals who desire to fulfill their responsibility as informal Christian witnesses—be permitted in any public welfare agency or service.

Questions and Paradoxes

We are long on opinions and short on facts about this subject. In order to find out the extent to which there actually are evangelistic motives, activities, and results in church-related social welfare, it would be necessary to conduct a careful and thorough research project. Such research should probe the intentions expressed by administrators, shared by workers, and perceived by clients. It should include evaluation to determine the extent to which the evangelistic and other goals are actually fulfilled. It might even attempt to assess the proportion of the impact that is evangelistic in relationship to the other effects of the actual ministries and services rendered.

It is likely that such investigations would reveal that direct evangelism is almost entirely absent from most types of church-related welfare agencies, but that indirect evangelism—proclamation or witnessing through deeds of love—is widespread. The actual evangelistic impact of such witness may be relatively slight, however, and it may be impossible to measure. It would be interesting to know how many patients in Baptist, Lutheran, and Catholic hospitals are converted as a direct result of hospital care. And how many new converts made their initial or early contacts with the church through its welfare programs? To what extent does "government surplus" food used in church camps and social service agencies contribute to evangelism and religious education?

Motives are always mixed. In regard to social welfare, they are so numerous and complex that it is very difficult to determine policies of church-state relationships on the basis of them. Perhaps a paradox similar to that of Baptist efforts on behalf of religious liberty will emerge on this topic of welfare also. Baptists want religious liberty because it is the condition under which their evangelistic opportunities are greatest. Working through governmental channels to extend religious liberty therefore becomes a form of using government to promote sectarian goals and thus constitutes a violation of the very principles they claim to support through that activity!

Research should also explore the relationships between motivations and theological positions. Perhaps the closer the theological position of an agency and its staff is to the fundamentalist end of the continuum, the more stress it will give to evangelism as a chief motive for social welfare; the closer it is to the theologically liberal end, the more emphasis there will be upon purely humanitarian service. Does this imply that government aid to theologically liberal religious welfare agencies and programs is consistent with church-state separation but public aid to conservative groups is not?

Notes

[1]Horace R. Cayton and Setsuko Matsunaga Nishi, *Churches and Social Welfare,* Vol. II: *The Changing Scene* (New York: National Council of the Churches of Christ in the U.S.A., 1955), p. 69.

[2]See, for example, George A. Kelly, "Man's Construction of His Alternatives," in Gardner Lindzey, ed., *Assessment of Human Motives* (New York: Rinehart and Co., 1958), pp. 33-64.

[3]Tamotsu Shibutani, *Society and Personality* (Englewood Cliffs, N. J.: Prentice-Hall, 1961), p. 77.

[4]Cayton and Nishi, *op. cit.,* p. 138.

[5]Dept. of Christian Social Ministries, "The Rescue Mission" (Atlanta, Ga.: Home Mission Board, Southern Baptist Convention, February 1967).

[6]Prof. E. E. Foelber, "The Scriptural Position with Reference to the Responsibility of the Church toward Welfare Work," reprinted from *Proceedings of Sixty-Third Convention of Central District* (St. Louis, Mo.: Dept. of Social Welfare, The Lutheran Church—Missouri Synod, 1940), pp. 23, 25.

[7]Alan Keith-Lucas, *The Church and Social Welfare* (Philadelphia: Westminster Press, 1962), pp. 12-13; see also pp. 18-32, 59-62.

[8]Cayton and Nishi, *op. cit.,* pp. 138, 139.

[9]*Ibid.,* pp. 139-143.

[10]Sue W. Spencer and Georgiana McLarnan, "The Religious Component in Social Work Practice," paper presented at the National Conference on Social Welfare, Cleveland, Ohio, May 21, 1963 (mimeographed), p. 10.

[11]Commission on the Role of the Church in Social Welfare, *The Church in Social Welfare* (New York: Board of Social Ministry, Lutheran Church in America, 1964), p. 73.

[12]E. Theodore Bachmann, ed., *Churches and Social Welfare,* Vol. III: *The Emerging Perspective* (New York: National Council of the Churches of Christ in the U.S.A., 1956), pp. 233-234.

[13]Commission on Evangelism, Lutheran Church in America, *Resource Book for Evangelism* (September 1960), Section V, pp. 3-4.

[14]Martin H. Scharlemann, "The Theological and Historical Basis for Lutheran Welfare," paper read at the Lutheran Social Work Institute, Valparaiso University, July 30-August 1, 1958 (mimeographed), p. 29.

[15]*Ibid.*, p. 27.

[16]Edward T. Hall, *The Silent Language* (Greenwich, Conn.: Premier Books, Fawcett Publications, 1964).

[17]The Rev. Joseph A. Pelham, "The Gospel and Social Service," *The Bulletin* (Anglican Church of Canada), No. 175 (March 1959), pp. 8, 9.

[18]E. Theodore Bachmann, ed., *Churches and Social Welfare*, Vol. I: *The Activating Concern* (New York: National Council of the Churches of Christ in the U.S.A., 1955), *passim.*

[19]Keith-Lucas, *op. cit.*, pp. 70-77; David O. Moberg, *Inasmuch:Christian Social Responsibility in the Twentieth Century* (Grand Rapids, Mich.: Eerdmans, 1965), pp. 155-157.

[20]Cayton and Nishi, *op. cit.*, p. 161.

[21]*Ibid.*, p. 165.

[22]*Ibid.*, pp. 128, 130.

[23]See Elizabeth L. Salomon, "Humanistic Values and Social Casework," *Social Casework*, Vol. 48, No. 1 (January 1967), pp. 26-32, and Donald F. Krill, "Existentialism: A Philosophy for Our Current Revolutions," *Social Service Review*, Vol. 40, No. 3 (September 1966), p. 301.

Social Sin   7

Mark Twain on December 12, 1900, introduced Winston
Churchill, then age twenty-six, who delivered a speech to
share his adventures in the Boer War in South Africa.
Twain spoke eloquently of himself as a self-appointed
missionary working for the cause of an alliance of the
heart of America with its Motherland. The two nations, he
said, were common in character, spirit, and deeds. They
always had been kin in blood, religion, representative
government, and ideals. Now, however, the harmony had
been completed, for "now we are kin in sin," and the
blend is perfected in the case of Mr. Churchill himself.[1]

But is it possible for sin to reside within a nation—not
just in the "hearts" of its citizens? Is not all sin individually committed, exclusively personal, and thus not a
social or collective phenomenon? And even when sin and
its results are apparent on a wide-scale basis, is it not
sufficient to approach its solution by an evangelistic effort
that calls guilty persons to repentance one by one?

Social Sin in the Old Testament

Only a brief look into a Bible concordance is needed to
reveal the prominence of social sin in the Old Testament.
Nations and peoples, tribes and families are condemned
collectively for their sins. Moral principles and proverbs
use collective nouns to proclaim that "Righteousness
exalts a nation, but sin is a reproach to any people" (Prov.
14:34).

Social Sin

Collective sin is evident in the numerous scriptural accounts in which an entire household or family is brought collectively under the judgment of God because of the wickedness of but one of its members. Children suffered for the transgressions of their fathers, citizens were punished for the evil deeds of their rulers, and young Israelites wandered unduly long in wilderness misery, kept out of the Promised Land because of the disobedience and murmuring of the older generation.

Idolatry, pride, seduction, greed, materialism, exploitation, slavery, and every additional form of sinfulness and man's inhumanity to man are compounded in the city, so God's judgment, condemnation, and curse are pronounced against all who are in it. The city, built as a place of refuge and the product of man's good will to protect, comfort, enrich, ennoble, and cheer him, becomes the place where bondage, suffering, unemployment, warfare, treating people like merchandise, slums, crime, prostitution, and all the other problems of mankind are heaped.[2]

God's punishment of Sodom and Gomorrah (Gen. 18:16–19:29) and numerous other cities and nations sweeps away the righteous individuals with the unrighteous. Social pressures are so strong that the group and its subculture draw men into sin that can hardly be labeled as personal, sin from which they cannot dissociate even if their individual virtues make them desire to do so.

For no one in the city has really committed a completely individual sin. No one, really, has individually violated, by his own decision, God's law or the order necessary to conserve life. But these men happen to be part of a body given entirely to revolt. They are not each individually responsible, but they are as a group. . . . What is characteristic of this type of sin is that no one commits it, but it is still committed. . . . This is what makes it impossible to pin down responsibility, for example, in wars or in social ills.[3]

The answer to social sin also is evident. As Jacques Ellul so eloquently explains, it is not enough simply to acquire new social structures or a new government. Neither is it adequate to repent as individual persons and begin to lead a pious, holy life. Jonah's experience with Nineveh reveals that only the conversion of an entire population, its government, and its other social, political, and spiritual structures can bring God's pardon. Social sin, the work of no single person but of all, is forgiven when a repentance occurs that is the work of all. Such repentance, of course, includes the individual act of each man as well as the collective act of the entire population. The solidarity in sin because of the structural solidarity of society and the acceptance of being condemned for actions one has not personally committed are recognized in genuine collective repentance. Nineveh is spared when it turns from idolatry in submission to God and is converted from its wicked ways.[4]

The theme of national repentance is accentuated today by Billy Graham and other evangelists who preach that, unless the nation repents, it will fall. They give casual observers the impression that the primary goal of their efforts is saving civilization's political structures; decisions for Christ by individuals are a means to the all-important end of preserving America.

Because of man's sinful inhumanity to man, God instructed the Israelites that every fiftieth year was to be a Year of Jubilee in which slaves were to be freed, debts canceled, and ancestral lands restored to their families (Lev. 25). Concern for protection of the poor and the oppressed is an equally similar concern of the "Jubilee King" who in Luke 4:18-19 declared social justice to be a major part of his ministry on earth. His followers will work for the liberation of all mankind from intolerable social conditions, racism, and socioeconomic exploitation.[5]

Social Sin in the New Testament

The New Testament, in general, gives a different first impression. The gospel is to be preached to every nation, and people are to be redeemed out of them all. God shows no partiality to the Jews; on the contrary, anyone from any nation who receives the good news of Jesus Christ and makes a faith commitment to Him will be saved. Many have assumed, therefore, that Christianity is an entirely individualistic religion which has no collective aspects.

The individualistic approach to religious questions fits the major themes of American culture very well, for the American nation has always been characterized by strong individualism. Accentuating it represents an excellent adaptation to the culture. Yet it also constitutes an example of the "conformity to the world" against which Christians are warned in passages like Romans 12:2.

In the great judgment when the Lord will return in His glory, all *nations* will be gathered before Him to be separated from one another as a shepherd separates the sheep from the goats (Matt. 25:31-46). Perhaps this speaks to collective as well as individual judgment in some mysterious way known to God but seen only dimly, and certainly not understood clearly, by me! Their eternal punishment or inheritance of the Kingdom will depend upon their social welfare activities of feeding the hungry, giving drink to the thirsty, welcoming strangers, clothing the naked, visiting the sick, and coming to the aid of prisoners.

Further examination of the New Testament reveals that Jesus taught His disciples to pray collectively, "Our

Father which art in heaven . . . ," not an individualistic prayer using singular pronouns. He built them together into a group which eventually became a church, a "body" in which were numerous members, each with personal gifts given by the Holy Spirit for the benefit of the collective whole (I Cor. 12; Rom. 12:4-8). In the Revelation of Jesus Christ to John the shortcomings of churches—not merely of individual members—were plainly identified (Rev. 2:1–3:22). Several later passages in Revelation refer to the sinfulness of nations. Just as Adam and Eve were involved in sin together, to the end of time people will sin collectively as well as individually.

Examples of Social Sin

Awareness of the reality of collective sin has grown considerably in recent decades. It has become clear that individual persons who are honest, kind, even God-fearing, may be implicated deeply in evil through their basic employment or their cooptation as citizens into national events over which they have but little direct control. Christians on both sides of modern wars have prayed for victory, feeling their side was the one of justice and righteousness which ought to receive God's blessing. Those on the winning side have felt that victory was God's vindication of their righteousness and the wickedness of their opponents; the vanquished have tended to feel that their loss represented but a temporary setback in the struggle of their righteous cause against the forces of evil. Can both be correct? Can either? If so, at least one side in the struggle was involved in social sin, even if it did not know it.

Today we view slavery as sinful. Were not the slave-holding Christians of ante-bellum America and all the businessmen, politicians, professors, and others who supported the social system of slavery involved in social sin? The same can be said about the inhumane aspects of child labor during the early stages of the industrial revolution, of cruel treatment of prisoners in the recent and distant past, of indignities heaped upon the mentally ill, of the exploitation of the poor through discriminatory employment practices, of the maltreatment of the mentally retarded, of the racial inequalities sustained while presumably living under "separate but equal" principles, and of numerous other injustices. A vicious cycle operates to perpetuate social evils and to prevent people from seeing them for what they really are. "It is the particular heresy of Americans that they see themselves as potential saints more than as real-life sinners."[6]

In Nazi Germany only a minority of Christians, now known as the "Confessing Church," were opposed to Hitler's regime and programs.[7] The majority believed church and state to be separate and autonomous realms; faithful Christians must be obedient to the state (Rom. 13:1-7), and the church must be neutral on political issues as long as it is free to preach the gospel and administer the sacraments. As a result, they complied with the suspension of civil liberties and failed to protest the persecution of Jews and Communists.[8] More than any other single set of events, this has awakened Christians to the fact that people within a nation may be honest, loyal, Christian citizens and yet support national evils which are a disgrace to mankind and a violation of the ethical teachings of the Christian Scriptures.

All human beings have a strong tendency to see evil only in others and only good in themselves, to find rationalizations (even from Bible passages, torn out of context if necessary) to justify their conduct, and to develop systematic social philosophies by which intellectual, political, and even religious support is given to their position. If a majority takes a stand, it must be right! The Prophet Jeremiah stated it well:

> The heart is deceitful above all things,
> and desperately corrupt;
> who can understand it? (Jer. 17:9)

Nor did Jesus hesitate to indicate that the majority is more likely to be wrong than right; He taught that many are walking the wide and easy road to destruction; only a minority are on the way that leads to life (Matt. 7:13-14). Moral, ethical, and religious issues settled by the majority vote of citizens are not at all certain to be without social sin.

Political Guilt

The typical Christian is a "good American" in his political behavior. He acts upon the American principle that each person and group ought to seek its own goals and, as each does so, out of it all will emerge a consensus for action that will constitute the greatest good for the greatest number. To put it very crassly in moralistic words, selfishness is the root principle of our political system.[9]

Americans selfishly assume that whatever is best for their own subculture, their own occupational group, their own neighborhood, city, state, or county, will obviously be best for the entire nation—indeed, for the entire world. The definition of "what is best" generally is along economic lines.

This perspective is in strong contrast to New Testament ethics which declare that we should love one another, put the interests of others ahead of our own selfish striving, bear one another's burdens, do good to all men, and even love our enemies and bless those who despitefully use us. Most Christians fail drastically to live up to such high standards in their political behavior. They are conformed to their culture and this world age, participating in its unrighteousness, condoning its social evils, and cooperating in its collective sin. Failing to do good is sin (James 4:17), as is all unrighteousness (I John 5:17). Such sins may be individual acts, or they may be acts indulged in by a family, a business, a volunteer association, a nation, or even a church. Continuing heedlessly and unrepentingly in such behavior is a symptom of "fractional conversion"; the condition of being converted to Jesus Christ in only part of one's life.[10]

The diffusion of the power of decision-making makes this an extremely complex subject. If the board of directors of a corporation makes a decision that is unjust or unkind to employees, harmful to customers, or destructive to the natural environment of its manufacturing plants, how much guilt is shared by the stockholders who have elected the board and to whom it is responsible? Typically, the majority of them give little attention to corporation decisions except those which affect dividends or the price per share of stock.

If the Congress of the United States passes a bill which causes suffering in some segment of the national or world population and the President signs it, to what extent and in what way do the citizens who have elected them share responsibility for the mixture of evil and good that results from its implementation? Do the members of the opposition party and voters who supported them share whatever guilt is involved? (Their taxes help pay the costs of the action.) Do those who acted with the majority believing in their hearts that they were doing good, perhaps even in faith believing they were fulfilling God's will, carry an equal share of guilt for the evil that results? (The foolish servant in Matthew 25:14-30 had good intentions when he protected his master's funds instead of investing them to increase his resources.)

The level of responsibility of each person apparently is in terms of the scope of the commitments placed in his charge (Luke 12:48). Such final judgment, however, is the prerogative of God. Meanwhile, the Christian's task is to test all things, firmly holding to whatever is good and avoiding every form of evil (I Thess. 5:21-22; Rom. 12:9; etc.).

Excuses for Social Sin

Men and women generally are self-justifying creatures. What would be called "sin" when observed in the conduct of someone outside one's own friendship group is likely to be only a "shortcoming," "deficiency," "weakness," "flaw," or "mistake" in one's own. Other speeders may be "law-breakers," but one's own violation of speed limits is merely "making good time." Others who cheat on income tax returns are "crooks," but to claim excess deductions for oneself is simply "saving money." Others who gossip "can't be trusted," but doing it oneself is simply "sharing some news." Others who use privileged political information to help friends make profitable investments are "influence peddlers" fleecing the public, but if we benefit from it, we only receive "a friendly tip."

We therefore are very hesitant to label undesirable conditions in our own society as "sins" unless we can trace them directly to sinful individuals or to personal vices that traditionally have been identified as sins. The precise listing of such "cardinal sins" among evangelical Protestants varies somewhat from one group to another, but typically they include drinking alcoholic beverages, using tobacco, social dancing, sexual immorality, gambling, and crimes against property or persons. Little attention is given to overeating, quarreling, jealousy, a party spirit, selfishness, conceit, prejudice ("respect of persons"), slander, and similar sins that are just as directly condemned in the Bible, nor to their manifestations in group life and activity. There is a strong attempt to attribute all social problems to the actions or inactions of individual persons; if a direct linkage of that kind is impossible, then we tend to excuse the causes away as impersonal and hence outside the range of Christian social ethics.

But God is the Lord of all creation. To "bug out" from any part of the stewardship responsibility that He has delegated to man is, in effect, to say that our faith is irrelevant to some portion of creation. To label injustices as merely coincidental by-products of doing good without seeing the way in which they violate the dignity of mankind created in the image of God, sustain human suffering, and in other ways contradict the verbal claim of being followers of God, who gives His good gifts to the unjust as well as to the just, is a form of denying the need to follow the example of Jesus Christ.

Good Intentions

It is difficult to accept the fact that good intentions may have evil results. The "increment of the apparent nothing" is a major source of the pollution of our air, waterways, underground water supplies, and landscape. What one person does is like nothing, but the "nothing" multiplied by thousands of littering persons, smoking planes, fuming automobiles, oily motorboat engines, and draining sewers threatens the ecological balance of the entire earth, causes many people to die prematurely, and may produce drastic results that cannot even be imagined at this time.[11]

With good intentions, the western prairies in the United States were ploughed during and after World War I to produce wheat for food, but the Dust Bowl developed despite the goodwill of those who caused it. With good intentions the American Indians were driven back from lands they had long occupied for their hunting, fishing, and pastoral economy and were herded into tiny areas especially "reserved" for them. With good intentions black people were captured by other blacks in Africa and sold for rum to traders who brought them to the West Indies where they were exchanged for sugar, which in turn was brought to New England to be manufactured into more rum for shipment to Africa on another leg of the nefarious three-cornered trade that made many families wealthy. Then with good intentions they were trained and sold into the United States to raise cotton—a noble goal, a product greatly needed. With good intentions the "robber barons" of American industry built their great corporations to provide products and services that were greatly needed in the rapidly developing nation while keeping wages inordinately low and giving little heed to working conditions until forced to do so by the rise of the labor movement.

There is considerable truth in the old proverb, "The road to hell is paved with good intentions." Intentions are not the criterion of what is good and what is evil. Many a criminal has had good intentions of helping the poor (himself or his family) by robbing the rich (his victim, whether economically rich or poor). Embezzlers typically have good intentions; they plan to pay the money back as soon as they "strike it rich" by gambling or speculative investments, or they take money that "no one would miss" in order to aid churches or other charitable causes. Medical doctors a century or two ago had good intentions when they drained "bad blood" from the bodies of the ill, but they caused many unnecessary deaths; the practice now is clearly not considered good medical practice, and it may even be a crime in some jurisdictions. Today the purchase of blood for transfusions is done with good intentions, but it apparently is becoming a major cause of the spread of diseases like hepatitis and may soon be classified as an evil to avoid.

Not intentions of the person who acts, but outcomes in the lives of people are major criteria of good or evil. Loving one's neighbor as one loves himself involves doing for fellow men what one would like done for oneself while keeping away from him conditions and experiences one would shun for oneself. Not intentions but effects are the key criteria of social as well as of individual evil.

Christians and Social Sin

To catalogue all of the social evils that prevail today in the world, or even in America, would be a tremendous task that is far beyond the scope of this book. It is easy to identify some of the currently popular issues by reading news magazines, "underground newspapers," and periodicals which devote attention to Christian social ethics. Numerous books devoted to the issues pour off the presses annually, and political speeches give clues, chiefly by their accusations against opposing candidates and parties. Many of these issues pertain to war—war crimes, atrocities, harm to civilians, treatment of prisoners, despoliation of forests and crops, R. O. T. C., war industries, the injustice of specific wars or of all wars, and similar topics. Others deal with discrimination against religious, racial, or other ethnic minorities, against women, against children, against welfare recipients, against the poor, against recent releasees from mental institutions, against parolees, or against other victims of real and alleged injustices. Current protest movements and groups pertain to pollution, the population explosion, restrictions upon the dissemination of birth-control information, anti-abortion legislation, the censorship of the mass media of communications, police brutality, jail and prison life, consumer fraud, funerary customs, and many other subjects. The precise issues that are popular targets at any given moment may vary widely from those given chief attention a few months earlier or later, so it is difficult to predict which will bear the brunt of popular attack in the future.

Some Christians assume that their churches must keep up with the times and be in the forefront of every specific movement to bring reform. To do so is impossible, at least on the local congregational or parish level, for the knowledge, time, and energy necessary to cover such a wide range of action intelligently and effectively is seldom if ever concentrated in any one place. Yet as citizens all Christians may be called upon to adopt positions on all of the issues, at least indirectly, by giving their electoral support to pertinent candidates and referenda. They must be aided to do so specifically as Christians; such help can come only through their churches and other religious associations. The reality of social sin, just as much as the reality of individual sin, therefore demands the attention of churches. Adult Christian education is needed more today than ever before, for society is changing so rapidly that the applications of Christian values learned in one decade may directly contradict their underlying principles if put into practice in another.

Social Sin

A division of labor by which some Christian groups focus upon the Christian response to certain categories of social evil while others focus upon different ones, all learning from the others and giving mutual support and encouragement to each other, may be a reasonable strategy for Christian social thought and action. Task forces within congregations, as well as some which draw together especially concerned or knowledgable people from numerous churches,[12] may be a contemporary adaptation of the principle that a variety of gifts and thus of responsibilities is found in the body of Christ (I Cor. 12).

Accurate interpretations and applications of Christian principles of faith, hope, love, justice, and stewardship can occur only if Christians specifically work on these issues with a conscious awareness of their vocation *as Christians,* while at the same time infusing all of their occupational, civic, recreational, consumptive, political, familial, and other roles with Christian values.[13] To do anything less is to capitulate to the sin of "fractional conversion."

Whose Side Will You Join?

One of the difficulties that deadens our vision of social sin is the complexity of social relationships. If we focus upon promoting the interests of any one group, we may gain considerable benefit for it without noticing the concomitant loss of another. Government programs that help the poor often take funds away from the rich through the compulsory power of taxation. Helping farmers by maintaining price supports for their products may harm consumers who as a result must pay higher prices for their food. Assisting industry through duties and tariffs on foreign products helps keep prices high, stimulates inflation, and reduces competition while also maintaining jobs for workers, so it has a mixed effect upon laborers and their families. Protecting the rights of law-abiding citizens against infringements upon due process of law also protects a few persons who have committed criminal acts. These examples could be multiplied indefinitely.[14]

In other words, what helps one group may harm another. No social problem affects all people equally; none can be resolved without economic, psychological, or other costs to some persons or groups, and these costs are never equally distributed. This is a part of the reality with which citizens must cope; it is a major source of the divergent political perspectives of faithful Christians. For whose interests should the Christian work in the socioeconomic and political conflicts that center around solving the human problems in a modern technological society which has a democratic form of government?

When there is doubt as to the group to support in the power struggles of society, many Christians throw up their hands in despair, assuming that no matter what they do, it will be wrong. Certainly any action will be wrong according to some groups, and usually even according to some Christians. But the more basic question goes back to the problem of what is right and wrong in the eyes of God as revealed in the Scriptures.

Personally, I have concluded after years of reflection upon this subject that the weight of Christians usually should be thrown behind the poor, dispossessed, outcast, strangers, and minorities of society. This conclusion has resulted from two major observations.

First of all, there is a great deal of attention to the poor in the Bible. Billy Graham in an address to Congressmen on behalf of the Poverty Program in the U.S. Office of

Economic Opportunity in 1967 indicated that this was the first time he had come to Washington to speak for or against a government program. He stated that he was a convert to the War on Poverty because of his intense study of both that program and the Bible. He had found 175 passages that command care for the poor and needy, "making anti-poverty efforts a major teaching of the Bible." The War on Poverty therefore should not become bogged down in partisan politics.[15]

Over and over again the Bible gives specific instructions to remember the poor and meet their needs, as well as to treat strangers fairly, help the weak, sustain those who suffer, and eradicate injustices that cause their grief. Far too often we spiritualize and thus explain away much of the direct, literal message of Jesus' quotation about Himself from Isaiah, stating that He was anointed by the Spirit of the Lord to minister to the poor, captives, blind, and oppressed (Luke 4:18-19). Furthermore, He was Himself despised and rejected by men, economically poor, and a man of sorrows acquainted with grief. People who are imitators of God, walking in the example of Christ's love (Eph. 5:1-2), must have a sincere and active concern for poor, suffering, and oppressed people. Such concern cannot be fulfilled adequately if attention is given only to the victims without also attempting to eliminate the causes which produce them in ever greater numbers.

A second basis for my conclusion that Christians should give special attention to the interests and needs of the poor and oppressed of society lies in the realities of our social structure. Those who have wealth are able to mobilize the resources of finances and personnel to sustain their power and retain their vested interests. They do not need our help. Indeed, they typically attempt to "buy" churchmen in order to strengthen and add to the other resources already at their disposal. Their selective giving to charitable, religious, and educational causes often reflects their support to agencies which perpetuate their power, sanction their privileged position, or sustain the status quo. When their self-centered interests are threatened from the pulpit, by church resolutions, or through social action programs, they wield the power of the purse by withholding their contributions. Today, as in the early church, Christians need to learn the lesson that showing partiality to certain people and their special interests is a sin (James 2:1-13); where it prevails, it is generally a collective sin in which a substantial body of people bow together before the throne of mammon.

Let us be thankful that there are exceptions; many of the rich have heeded the admonition the Apostle Paul passed on to the young minister, Timothy:

> As for the rich in this world, charge them not to be haughty, nor to set their hopes on uncertain riches but on God who richly furnishes us with everything to enjoy. They are to do good, to be rich in good deeds, liberal and generous, thus laying up for themselves a good foundation for the future, so that they may take hold of the life which is life indeed (I Tim. 6:17-19).

"Who speaks for the poor?" is a question that echoes throughout the world. They seldom have opportunity and, if given it, frequently lack the ability to speak effectively for themselves. As a result, the "trickle down" theory prevails in numerous areas of social life; it is assumed that by helping the rich, one will help the poor. The trickle attenuates, however, at each of its falls on the cascade of socioeconomic status, and the drops that eventually reach the lowest of the poor are few and long deferred. The realities of this form of social injustice need much greater attention from social scientists and Christian social ethicists than they have received to this date. If Christians do not speak for the poor, who will?

Protest Movements

Although it is seldom expressed and explained in the foregoing manner, much of the protest movement is a reaction against the failure of "the establishment" to recognize their implication in social evils. That societal disruptions, defects, disorganization, deviance, discrimination, and dissension are indigenous to modern society and that injustice, inequities, and irregularities are widespread cannot be denied by anyone who has studied the social sciences, nor even by those who simply follow the news of current events. The fact that society is like a great network or web of social relationships and structures means that it is impossible to bring about major changes in any segment of it without affecting all the other parts. Just as the fly alighting on a spider's web makes the entire web quiver, so the problems of any minority group or subculture shake all of society.

The entire nation is implicated in all of its problems. When minority groups begin to feel that those who have power to bring about changes are refusing to deal with certain key issues or are incapable of doing so, they tend to lose faith in the ability or willingness of the "power structure" to cope with other needs for social order and justice as well. The result is a strong negative reaction against every vested interest and power figure and a call for total revolution in the assumption that any alternative whatever, including anarchy, is better than the present state of affairs. The ideals of alternative socioeconomic and political philosophies may be joyfully received, with a failure to realize that the ideals, like those undergirding our own social system, are seldom attained in fact.

Perceptions of the situation may deviate widely from reality, but men respond in terms of their images or definitions of a situation, so the consequences of false images may be very real. When people believe that our present social system is hopelessly bogged down in injustice, they tend either to become radical revolutionaries attempting to overthrow it entirely or to adopt a monastic type of response by which they attempt like Pilate to wash their hands of all responsibility.

When youthful and other radicals see religious institutions giving their direct or indirect blessing to the status quo, they interpret this as sanctioning the social evil that is a part of the web of societal life even if the leaders who do so interpret their action as a benediction only of the good therein. Charges of hypocrisy, insincerity, deception, pretense, duplicity, and pharisaism against the churches grow out of these perceived inconsistencies. Meanwhile it is easy for religious leaders, as well as for those who are members of the political, economic, and other power structures of society, to identify the hypocrisies and inconsistencies in the lives of their critics.

Each side in the ideological struggle is reacting to a partial picture of the total situation. Each compares its own ideals with the actualities of the other. In both instances social sin is a major component of the battle. It must be dealt with by Christians and, above all, by those who strongly rely upon the Bible as their guide to faith and conduct.

Revolution

In a fluent statement on the relationships between religion and politics, Senator Mark Hatfield has indicated that many on both the political Left and the Right "believe that politics is an inevitably corrupting practice that deserves little regard, if not downright contempt."[16] Similarly, many may not quite believe that religion is the opiate of the people but consider it as "not much more than pablum as far as politics is concerned."[17] How to live in two worlds creates problems for Christian politicians which are also the problems of all Christian citizens in a democratic society.

One of these problems pertains to the question of whether to support or oppose the radical changes in societal structures which are called for by numerous movements and prophetic spokesmen. From both within and outside of Christian contexts they prophetically call the nation to repent by making a clean sweep of current social organizations and practices.

The right to revolt against an unjust government is built into some of the most hallowed traditions of the United States of America. The Declaration of Independence includes these words following its expression about self-evident truths and the purpose of government:

That whenever any Form of Government becomes destructive of these ends, it is the Right of the People to alter or to abolish it, and to institute new Government, laying its foundation on such principles and organizing its powers in such form, as to them shall seem most likely to effect their Safety and Happiness.

Perhaps most Americans no longer believe that Declaration, now two centuries old, although they would certainly say they believe in "the principles of the Declaration of Independence" if these precise principles were not specifically mentioned!

The seed of the political philosophy of the right of revolution is also implanted through the significant influence of the traditions of ancient Israel upon America. Their judges and kings ruled by appointment from God. When their misconduct violated God's commandments through some breach of the personal trust and relationships between God and man or between man and man, they were condemned for violation of God's law. The people could appeal to God for protection and justification in seeking relief from an evil or oppressive ruler through altering or overthrowing the unjust government. At the same time, however, suffering under such rulers was often interpreted as a direct punishment of God for the evil conduct of the people in their disobedience to God's commandments. The "corrupt and evil government resulted from the moral degeneration of the people themselves."[18]

Today we seldom see government's relationships to religion in such stark and naked clarity. Not only are they garbed in centuries more of tradition, which politically has major infusions of Greek and Roman values, but they also are veiled by the multiplicity of philosophies and religions which characterize our pluralistic society. Nevertheless, there are important linkages on the institutional level (church and state, welfare agencies and volunteer societies, schools and families) as well as on the personal level in which individual citizens simultaneously are members of both the religious and the political realms of human activity. Because the Christian faith infuses all of life, church and state, the sacred and the secular, religion and politics all converge in the individual person. Revolutionary implications of complete commitment to Jesus Christ affect one's political and social involvements.

American Christians today live in a society of rapid change. Change is so rapid and significant that Jean-François Revel believes the revolution of the twentieth century has already begun to occur in the United States and will sweep from it to the rest of the world. It is sparked by the new revolutionary method of dissent, and in America it is occurring without dogmatic reference to traditional formulas, whether of Marx or Jesus, for building a better world.[19] The New Left is working for revolutionary change, not simply reform, of the entire social system. It is trying to live as if the revolution already has come, not merely attempting a patchwork of the present system.[20]

Change is inevitable; the greater the degree to which those who hold power in society resist it and hold on to their privileged position, the greater is the likelihood that it will come violently. Change that is fundamental, affecting the basis of civilization itself, is revolutionary. In this age in which our social system is leading to a new form of enslavement which, by impersonal relationships, centralized decision-making, and many controls, tends to reduce man to an object, revolution is greatly needed. Christians "should accept the collapse of the old and welcome the signs of a new order."[21] To be obedient to Christ, one must be a revolutionary.

But this is to not say that any and all change is desirable. Some changes are destructive, producing greater injustices than those they were intended to eliminate. On the other hand, to refuse to work for change designed to eliminate evil from society is to perpetuate its organized systems of exploitation, oppression, cruelty, and hypocrisy.

The obedient Christian will not compromise his vision of a new society and a new humanity by siding unequivocably with either the revolutionaries or their opponents. He will work on the levels of both personal and social sin and salvation. He hopes for the conversion, not the annihilation, of his opponents as he witnesses to what God already has done and what He yet will do.

When a Christian is faithful to Christ and refuses compromise with the demands of society, it is almost inevitable that he will be looked upon by the power structures of that society as being disloyal and subversive, and so he is. He is a person who dares to call the whole society into question. He is a revolutionary.[22]

It is tragic that the only revolutions accepted with respect by most Christians are those of the past. Perhaps they are so squeezed into the mold of conformity with the present world age, which has been shaped by past revolutions, that they absolutize, perhaps even idolize, it. One is tempted to believe the saying, "A conservative is someone who worships a dead radical."

In contrast, the Christian who is obedient to his heavenly vision will not capitulate to the absoluteness of any earthly system or authority.[23] He will not arbitrarily assume that all social, economic, and political revolutions are necessarily evil. Instead of siding with the power structure by assuming a stance of neutrality, he will recognize the inevitability of revolution, seek to understand its causes, declare his sympathy for the oppressed and demonstrate it by acts of compassion, proclaim the judgment of God against all evil and oppression, and seek to inculcate a passion for righteousness among all people at every level of society. His scriptural drive for both social righteousness and individual holiness will produce wholesome results in the area of social action as well as in social welfare and evangelism.[24] His "revolutionary

evangelism" will "combine the prophets, who called for
repentance and justice, with the apostles, who called for
repentance and faith in Jesus Christ."[25]

Evangelism Is Part of the Solution

I sympathize deeply with those evangelicals who react
against the concept of corporate guilt for social evils.
There is validity to the argument that assigning responsibility on a collective basis is a "copout." It easily leads
to the assumption that no individual can do anything
about the problems, hence it is no use to waste the effort
of trying to bring about change. If all are guilty, no one is
responsible. It also can be a rationalization, serving as a
balm for any hidden feelings of guilt that individual
participants may have; their share in the decision-making
process is so indirect and small that they certainly cannot
be counted among the guilty.

Christians, however, are expected to be the salt of the
earth. Some are tempted to give up this responsibility by
saying that it is of no use to try to control the festering
sores and the rotting decay of society or by claiming that
Christian concern lies solely in the realm of individual
soul-winning because people are saved only for the
purpose of winning others. To do so is to withdraw the
benefits of the salt from society; if the salt has lost its
beneficial powers, it is good only to be cast out to be trod
underfoot by men (Matt. 5:13). The disrespect many
people have for the social perspectives of theologically
conservative Christians can be traced largely to their
default in regard to the problems related to social sin. Yet
it must also be remembered that salt grains generally are
unobserved and unobservable, at least to the naked eye,
when they are performing their preserving, healing, and
other functions.

One reaction to the evangelical default ever since the

Great Reversal has been an overemphasis upon social ministries in many Christian organizations. Accepting the false dichotomy of evangelism and social concern, they have swung to the pole of the continuum opposite to soul-winning and engaged in social reconstruction as "a new form of evangelism," giving up all efforts to deal with the needs of individual persons. The resulting dilemmas, problems, and schismatic divisions have already been noted in earlier chapters.

Evangelism is relevant to social evil on the societal and structural as well as the personal level. First of all, the victims of social evil will not hear the words of the gospel if they are so caught up in suffering that it preoccupies their thoughts, energy, and time. A cynical cartoon a few years ago portrayed a man wearing clerical garb sitting in a rowboat on a body of water with no land in sight. He was reading a black book decorated on the cover with a large cross. From the deep waters beside the boat a hand appeared, stretched out for help. The next panel portrayed the cleric with a peaceful smile placing the book in the drowning man's hand.

To "rescue the perishing, care for the dying" calls for much more than a verbalized message of the gospel. It demands a demonstration of love that meets immediate felt needs in addition to the proclamation of God's love which is communicated best of all by the Living Word, Jesus Christ. Serving the victims of social problems *in the name of Jesus Christ* is an essential component of effective evangelism.[26]

Precisely *how* to serve in Jesus' name will vary with the specific situation, of course. Standing aloof in a "Lady Charity" attitude of "slumming" in order to give tidbit handouts of help from an exalted position of social eminence will frequently produce negative reactions, although genuine compassion may develop most effectively of all only when there is personal interaction with those who suffer because of housing discrimination, unemployment, poverty, or other social problems. Recognition of the necessity for social reforms often results from efforts to satisfy welfare needs.[27]

Helping the victims of social problems and corporate evil is not the same as eliminating the sources of their misery. The floodwaters that sweep them off their feet and cause them to drown must be cut off or diverted at their source; otherwise the victims will increase more rapidly than those who are rescued. Reforms in society are essential in order to correct dehumanizing inequities, eliminate injustice, and eradicate all violations of basic human rights. To bring about reform is to introduce change; those who have vested interests of property, power, or prestige will tend to oppose any changes that threaten their special privileges. Many of them are church members. The natural deceitfulness of the mind of man will make them selectively emphasize biblical teachings and Christian values in support of their vested interests in the status quo and blind them to noticing those which stand in opposition. Thus their selective "proof-texting" of the Bible provides a "Christian" rationale which opposes social change.

Added to this problem is the "power of the purse," which operates strongly in numerous churches. The contributors of large sums of money are often heeded in far greater proportion during church-planning decisions than their "equals in Christ" who lack financial means. They also are benefactors of their ministers, taking them out to the country club for dinner or golf or bringing them along on distant hunting or fishing trips. Frequent association with a given type of people tends to modify social beliefs and perspectives. Many clergymen are subtly influenced to give special heed to but one set of value orientations as a result of greater social interaction with the wealthy than with the poor among their members—if indeed there are any of the latter in their middle-class congregations.

The influence of the privileged classes also is evident in churches in other subtle ways. They are the most likely to have had extensive higher education, to be organizationally experienced, to be fluent communicators, and thus to be effective leaders. They therefore tend to be elected in disproportionate numbers to church offices, presidencies of church-related organizations, and the boards of denominationally affiliated service agencies. It is they who have the necessary communication skills, financial resources, and ability to adjust their own time schedules on their jobs to enable service as delegates to denominational conventions at which resolutions and other recommendations about social issues are made.[28] Without deliberate intent on the part of church leaders, those who hold the greatest amount of power in society thus tend also to wield a disproportionate amount of power in religious institutions. Their influence in opposition to social changes which would modify the power structure tends to be felt strongly in churches, which as a result usually are more strongly inclined toward perpetuating the status quo than toward changing it. They need to be converted.

Even Christian members of the various power structures of our pluralistic society may not be able as individual persons to bring about much change, but, by the interstimulation that comes while working with others as civic leaders, council members, directors, and advisors in various types of business, governmental, religious, educational, and other voluntary associations, they can be the salt and light of the world. To serve in that capacity, instead of for merely self-centered goals, however, necessitates dying daily to the old nature and living a life of true discipleship motivated by a love for God and for others that can come through Christian conversion and growth in Christian maturity.

The motivation to love, the values to guide ethical-moral decisions, the openness to see the perspectives of others, and the willingness to consider their interests in political and other decisions are all necessary for correcting and eliminating corporate evil. These can come through effective Christian evangelism when it is accompanied by the nurture of biblically grounded education, worship, and social interaction.

Without evangelism most efforts to restructure society will fail.

Notes

[1]"'Now We Are Kin in Sin . . . '," *American Heritage,* Vol. XII, No. 5 (August 1961), p. 112.

[2]Jacques Ellul, *The Meaning of the City,* Dennis Pardee, trans. (Grand Rapids, Mich.; Eerdmans, 1970), pp. 44-62.

[3]*Ibid.,* p. 67.

[4]*Ibid.,* pp. 66-70.

[5]James B. White, "Jubilee: The Basis of Social Action," *The Reformed Journal,* Vol. XXI, No. 5 (May-June 1971), pp. 8-11.

[6]"On Evil: The Inescapable Fact," *Time,* Vol. XCIV, No. 23 (December 5, 1969), p. 27.

[7]Hans Heinrich Wolf, "Barmer theolog. Erklaerung," in Friedrich Karrenberg, ed., *Evangelisches Soziallexikon* (Stuttgart: Kreuz-Verlag, 1954), p. 138.

[8]Roger Mehl, *The Sociology of Protestantism,* James H. Farley, trans. (Philadelphia: Westminster Press, 1970), pp. 273, 278-279.

[9]The same is probably true of every other political system, so this statement must not be misinterpreted as indicating that I advocate overthrow of our form of government!

[10]Theologically this may be impossible; either one is depending upon

Jesus Christ for eternal life or he is not. But sociologically there are many degrees of growth in Christian maturity; the person who insists that his faith is completely irrelevant to his daily activities can be considered as converted only fractionally. The compartmentalizer, who assumes he has a Christian role when in church but other roles elsewhere or who divides his "sacred" from his "secular" life, is but one of many varieties of the "fractionally converted."

[11]See Garrett Hardin, "The Tragedy of the Commons," *Science,* Vol. CLXII (1968), pp. 1243-1248.

[12]The Shaftesbury Project sponsored by Inter-Varsity Fellowship in England is an excellent current example of an evangelical effort organized along such lines.

[13]See Elton Trueblood, *Your Other Vocation* (New York: Harper & Brothers, 1952).

[14]These are all oversimplified and should not be interpreted as having any broader purpose here than to serve as mere illustrations. Every one of them is so complex that any positional statement needs elaborate qualification and clarification.

[15]Phillip Hardberger, "The Moral War," *Communities in Action,* Vol. II, No. 5 (October-November 1967), pp. 4-5.

[16]Mark O. Hatfield, *Conflict and Conscience* (Waco, Tex.: Word Books, 1971), p. 148 (italics removed).

[17]*Ibid.*

[18]*Ibid.,* p. 151.

[19]Jean-François Revel, *Without Marx or Jesus* (Garden City, N. Y.: Doubleday and Co., 1971).

[20]Arthur G. Gish, *The New Left and Christian Radicalism* (Grand Rapids, Mich.: Eerdmans, 1970), pp. 40-47.

[21]*Ibid.,* p. 119.

[22]*Ibid.,* p. 113. See also Vernon C. Grounds, *Revolution and the Christian Faith* (Philadelphia: J. B. Lippincott, 1971), an analysis of the theology of revolution made as a contribution to the cause of Jesus Christ, "that redemptive revolutionary"; and "Would You Have Signed the Declaration of Independence? Sixteen Experts Examine the Christian's Response to the Cry of 'Revolution!'" *Eternity,* Vol. XXII, No. 7 (July 1971), pp. 18-24.

[23]*Ibid.,* pp. 113-142. Some of Jesus' actions were "revolutionary," but others seemed to defend the status quo; actually, He went beyond both the revolutionary and reactionary positions and refused to attribute eternal worth to any existing institution (James M. Boice, "Was Jesus a Revolutionary?" *Eternity,* Vol. XXIII, No. 2 [February 1972], pp. 20-22).

[24]Horace L. Fenton, "Missions and Revolution," *Latin American Evangelist,* Vol. XLIX, No. 2 (March-April, 1969), pp. 3-5.

[25]Evangelist Leighton Ford, as quoted by Terence Shea, "Controversy on the Sawdust Trail: Call to 'Revolutionary Evangelism' Shakes a Traditional Ministry," *The National Observer,* Vol. VIII, No. 37 (September 15, 1969) p. 4.

[26]See Matt. 18:5; Mark 9:39-41; John 15:21; Rev. 2:3; 3:8; etc.

[27]Stephen C. Mott, "From Another Perspective," *Inside,* Vol. II, No. 1 (January 1971), pp. 14-19.

[28]David O. Moberg, *The Church as a Social Institution* (Englewood Cliffs, N. J. : Prentice-Hall, 1962), pp. 147-149.

Reversing the Great Reversal

Ever since the Great Reversal which separated evangelism from the Social Gospel during the controversies between fundamentalists and modernists early in this century, the false dichotomy between evangelism, which stresses personal salvation, and social concern, which emphasizes the regeneration of society, has hampered the work and witness of evangelicals and other Protestants.

The problem is parallel to other paradoxical issues in contemporary society, such as the recurring question in social work about "the extent to which objectives that deal with social reform and social change can be harmonized with objectives that are directed primarily towards helping the individual."[1] Just as the social worker is under pressure to choose between the individual and society as a client, the Christian is tempted to believe that he can effectively cover the entire range of human need and implement the full scope of the gospel by focusing upon a ministry either to persons as individuals or to men collectively as society.

This chapter summarizes our conclusions about the ideal relationships between evangelism and social concern, basing our judgment of that set of values upon biblical teachings and principles, and surveys recent developments in evangelicalism which are reversing the Great Reversal.

Part One: Ideals

In Chapter 1 we presented two "ideal types" or alternative Christian approaches to human need, those of "evangelism" and "social involvement." In subsequent chapters we have dealt with various topics pertinent to these approaches. Let us first summarize the relative strengths and weaknesses of the two contrasting forms of Christian action. Then we will present an alternative solution to the dilemma which has entrapped the followers of both extremes.

An Evaluation of the Polar Positions

The evangelistic approach in its idealistic form is good. It is true that *if* all people on earth were converted to Jesus Christ, and *if* all who were converted would fully conform to God's will for their lives, *then* all evil in our social institutions and processes would be eradicated. But even the most zealous soul-winner cannot realistically foresee a day before Christ's return when everyone on earth will acknowledge Him as Savior and Lord. Furthermore, everyone continues to sin even after conversion (I John 1:8), so not even the most devout person is perfectly pure and holy in all of his relationships, thoughts, and actions. No one on earth is, in this sense, "one hundred percent converted."

Christians still are being saved. They are only in the process of growing toward "mature manhood, to the measure of the stature of the fullness of Christ" (Eph. 4:13). They have not yet arrived. The utopian goal of changing the world through soul-winning alone is hence a sincere but visionary excuse for evading Christian social responsibility. So is the plea that we should wait for the coming of Christ's Kingdom instead of working for it.

Meanwhile, however, the social-action approach also is limited, as even the best of the social gospelers acknowledged:

> It is true that any regeneration of society can come only through the act of God and the presence of Christ; but God is now acting, and Christ is now here. To assert that means not less faith, but more. It is true that any effort at social regeneration is dogged by perpetual relapses and doomed forever to fall short of its aim. But the same is true of our personal efforts to live a Christ-like life; it is true, also, of every local church, and of the history of the Church at large. Whatever argument would demand the postponement of social regeneration to a future era will equally demand the postponement of personal holiness to a future life.[2]

The social-action approach must therefore be linked with evangelism. Regenerate persons pledged to a life of righteousness and holiness are a most important source of social reform. Regeneration creates the will to do what is right and good, loving and just. It provides the motivation of love to serve the interests of one's neighbor as well as those of oneself.

Evangelism and social concern are reciprocally linked in a number of ways. To see them as separate and antithetical is to be caught up in the false dichotomies that so often paralyze the Christian life and witness. It is not necessary to choose between the social and the personal aspects of the gospel; both are important. We are not required to select between this-worldliness and otherworldliness, for salvation relates to both. We are not forced to choose to follow either the secular or the spiritual implications of the Christian message, for both are validly present. We are not compelled to cast our lot with those who believe in the brotherhood of Christians only or with those who believe in the brotherhood of man, for both, properly delimited and rightly understood, are biblical doctrines. It is not necessary to choose between political compromise and the purity of non-involvement, for the former may be less sinful than dogmatic firmness, and the latter is usually not pure. We do not need to decide either to wait for the coming of Christ or to work until His coming, for both have their place. We are not required to choose between separation from the world and association with sinners, for both are important (see I Cor. 5:9-10).

False alternatives like these have blinded men in each camp to the validity of truths emphasized by the other. God's will for their lives has been seen only partly by those who have been trapped into the either-or position of viewing social concern and evangelism as horns of a dilemma.

The Biblical Balance

The fracturing impact of polarized thinking that compels Christians to believe that they must be either *activists,* who attack entrenched social evils, or *pietists,* who emphasize the life of prayer, worship, devotion, and personal evangelism, can be overcome only by the realization that both perspectives are important. Pietism and activism are interdependent. Pietism is the root of the Christian life and activism its fruit.[3]

Expressed in other words:

A church that sets out to do the works of God, spreading into every area of life, yet neglecting the living center of belief, is doomed not to renewal, but to decay. The passion to do the works of God must be inspired and controlled by a stronger and deeper belief.[4]

153

Analysis of the single word *salvation* as used in the Bible establishes beyond a shadow of doubt that Christians do have a social responsibility. To try to prove that they do is "tantamount to a statistical survey demonstrating that all husbands are married. . . . the Christian religion is inconceivable apart from its social teachings."[5]

The validity of this balanced perspective is confirmed by the lessons Dr. Howard Hageman learned in his twenty-four years of experience as pastor of the North Reformed Church in inner city Newark, New Jersey. He has found that attempts to evangelize the inner city have been paralyzed because some concentrate strictly on evangelism, leaving "social work" to secular groups, while others attempt to improve social conditions but fail to follow it up with a presentation of the gospel. Instead of working together, the two kinds of efforts cancel each other out. Both are necessary to bring Jesus Christ into the inner city to resolve its problems.[6]

The false dichotomy which assumed that Christians may be involved in either preaching the Good News or working to improve social conditions has played havoc in Christendom. Jesus ministered to the whole man; His compassion moved Him to both physical and spiritual ministries; those who make Him Lord will act similarly.

Christians should therefore be taught to *do* those actions which promote the good of all men. Christians should act on behalf of justice and righteousness in the social and political spheres and *not* neglect proclaiming salvation through the reconciling death of the God-Man, Jesus Christ.[7]

Conversion to Jesus Christ creates the motivation or will to do right, but it does not in itself define for any person precisely *what* is right.[8] That training is a major task of the church—and it is no secret that most churches, whether theologically liberal, neo-orthodox, evangelical, or fundamentalistic, have not performed that task very well. This failure is especially apparent in the area of race relations in which a racist attitude of "enlightened apathy" prevails among most whites. On this, as on other issues, "Christians in America have shown an almost unfailing ability to be comfortably assimilated into the American way of life, much like an insignificant piece of a giant jigsaw puzzle."[9] The "compassion fatigue" and "conscience sickness" of the American nation deeply afflict Christians. They have caused an inability to respond to the stimuli of problems of hunger, disease, and poverty, if not also an immunity against awareness of their existence.[10]

Too many Christians have failed to recognize the full import of the Great Commission of Jesus Christ. They emphasize the evangelistic and missionary commands of its first three instructions (to go, make disciples, and baptize them), but they totally overlook the fourth, "teaching them to observe all that I have commanded you" (Matt. 28:20). It is here that Christian social concern lies. Above all else, the Lord's commands emphasize a balance of both loving God and loving one's neighbor as he loves himself (Luke 10:27). To be a neighbor, Jesus explained through the story of the Good Samaritan, is to show mercy upon anyone who needs compassion and love.

The example of Jesus Christ, obedience to God's will as revealed throughout the Scriptures, Christ's judgment of the nations, explanations of the works of love and the fruit of the Spirit in passages like I Corinthians 12 and Galatians 5, and the exemplary love of God shown to the unrighteous, the unworthy, and the irresponsible all clarify what is meant by observing all that Christ commanded.[11] He calls for the best of each camp—both evangelism and social concern.

Evangelistic Christians are quick to quote Ephesians 2:8-9 about the free gift of salvation, but they tend to overlook the verse that follows: "For we are his workmanship, created in Christ Jesus for good works, which God prepared beforehand, that we should walk in them."

Meanwhile, socially involved Christians who emphasize that Christians are the light of the world and the salt of the earth (Matt. 5:13-16) tend to forget that non-Christian men who see their good works will not give glory to God unless these works are accompanied by the communicated message that the good deeds are a result of the love of Christ, that "We love, because he first loved us" (I John 4:19). People will not ask one to account for the hope that is in him if they have never heard of his hope (I Pet. 3:15)! But when "acts of love" are without the dissimulation of ulterior motives (such as being merely "bait" to win converts), the deeds of kindness are sermons even when no advertising "commercial" is attached to the specific act.

Any "love for others" that is merely "in the heart" without any outward expression is not love at all. True love always involves deeds, not just devotion; activity, not just attitudes; works, not just worship; facts, not just faith. (Study I Cor. 13 and James 2!) Any "love for souls" that neglects the body is a perversion seeking selfish rewards. The world is quick to see the inconsistencies of those who come with the words of a gospel of love but lack the support of loving deeds. The rebellion of many American youth against the faith of their fathers, and even such great historical events as the Russian Revolution, can be traced in part to such inconsistencies.

Reciprocal Relationships

Socially oriented Christians who try to reform society sometimes do so for only thinly cloaked, self-centered reasons. They also tend to overlook the necessity of changing the value orientations of people who hold key positions in the power structures of society as a most important prerequisite for and component of social change. As long as the power elite, together with the voters who support them politically, consumers who enrich them economically, stockholders who insist that they produce high yields on investments, and others who give them authority, wealth, and power, are selfishly oriented, they will resist reforms to correct the numerous structural defects of society. Unless they are converted from their greedy, self-centered grasping for wealth, status, and power, major social reforms will not occur.

Personal regeneration that brings new self-conceptions and an orientation of love for God and others, not only for oneself, is therefore essential to social regeneration. Social morality on both the personal and collective levels will flow out of lives transformed by God's grace if and when they are helped to grow in their knowledge of the complex nature of human problems and in the wisdom, grace, and love of their Lord and Savior, Jesus Christ.[12] The social sciences can help to play a Christian prophetic role by enlightening us about society, its strengths and weaknesses, its virtues and hypocrisies, its discrepancies between ideals and action, and similar information. The motivation of Christian commitment provides the compelling drive of love to act upon the basis of social science knowledge and Christian ethics. Effective social reform therefore is tightly linked with effective evangelism.

Through social action the historic goals of the Christian church can be concretized; when the historic goals are properly emphasized, social responsibilities will become clear.[13] This is probably a major reason for Edward C. Lehman's finding that among university faculty members there is a direct relationship between degree of personal religious commitment and perception of the relevance of traditional religion to selected social issues. The more involved the professors were, the more likely they were to view traditional religion as socially relevant.[14] When people's spiritual eyes are opened, they become aware of Christian social responsibility.

An active social concern also can do much to promote evangelism. It demonstrates what love is so that people learn by example and by experience what is meant by the love of God; they cannot respond to verbal accounts of God's love if they do not know the operational definition of what love is. Social ministries remove the barriers of hunger, pain, anxiety, and other economic, physical, psychological, and social problems which otherwise prevent many people from truly hearing the gospel when the message of Christ is spoken to them. Christian social concern plants and waters seeds of the gospel that in due time will yield their increase, as some of the seed falls on fertile ground and is watered well.

Fulfilling Christian social responsibility is in itself a form of evangelism. Social welfare to treat the victims of human problems and social action to prevent or ameliorate their future occurrence not only help remove barriers from hearing the evangelistic message, but they also constitute a message from God whenever they are done "in Jesus' name."

Christians communicate God's love by deeds as well as by words. Just as it was necessary for the Living Word to become flesh and dwell among men in order that they might behold "his glory, glory as of the only Son from the Father" (John 1:14), full of grace and truth, so our message must become incarnate in our deeds. We teach by doing, even more than by speaking. Demonstrating acceptance of the sinner through welfare and other social action communicates the love of God, Who loves men as they are, even when they are dead in trespasses and sins. The positive, consistent life of the Christian layman who faithfully fulfills his daily tasks of serving others in his work and in his neighborhood is a potent evangelistic instrument.

When a church engages in social action and social services, community leaders and agency representatives become aware of its existence. They become favorably disposed toward it, are more likely to listen when its leaders speak to public issues, will refer people with spiritual problems to its ministries, may turn to the Christian for help in times of personal need, and are more likely to open their minds to give favorable consideration to the claims of Christ in their own lives.

Social concern thus promotes evangelism, while evangelism gives people new motivations, a new outlook on life, new self-concepts, and a new set of values that helps them to change their goals, their manner of living, and their social, economic, and political behavior. Evangelism thus contributes to the implementation and fulfillment of social concern.

Part Two: Actualities

In Chapter 2 we noted that evangelical Christianity was a major influence on many social reforms in the eighteenth and nineteenth centuries, but the Great Reversal early in this century led them to react against social involvement, partly because it was identified with a lopsided Social Gospel. They also assumed that their total responsibility to their fellow men was fulfilled by evangelism, a few welfare activities, and the presumably automatic responses of individual Christians to needs for political and socioeconomic action. Instead of being in the forefront of social concern, evangelicals reverted to the position of being at the tail end of nearly every effort to bring about social reform.

I am glad, however, that a new voice is increasingly heard among evangelicals, a voice that is much closer to the mind and heart of the Lord Jesus Christ. It does not say in one breath, "When all people are saved, social problems will be solved, so our task is to control social problems through evangelism," and then in the next, "The majority are walking the broad road to destruction and always will." It is more consistent with the Scriptures and more consistent with social-science knowledge about current society. It is not based upon such illusionary goals as the attempt to "re-establish" an idyllic rural society that never existed in the first place. If its message is heeded, evangelicals will once again be known for their forward look instead of for their foot-dragging and backwardness about the needs of men in contemporary society.

The Renewal of Evangelical Social Concern

The first widely heard spokesman calling for a revival of interest in social issues was Carl F. H. Henry, who exposed "the uneasy conscience of modern fundamentalism" and called for a "new reformation" which would make clear the implications of personal regeneration for social as well as individual problems.[15] Since then there has been an ever-increasing flow of articles, sermons, books, and resolutions dealing with social issues from evangelical perspectives. Beginning with a tiny trickle, it reached the proportions of a small stream in the late 1960's and promises to become a mighty river of evangelical social concern during the 1970's.[16]

Some of this work presents a relatively traditional emphasis upon personal regeneration and individual action as the basic means of solving the problems of society, but attention also is increasingly given to the limitations of individualistic approaches to complex social issues, and a call for "Christian radicalism" emerges from some.[17] It is recognized that, in order to deal scripturally and effectively with the needs of men in contemporary society, their social settings as well as the Bible must be studied. As evangelical social and behavioral scientists gain the attention and respect of fellow Christians, we can expect the proclamations and other actions of theologically conservative Christians to be increasingly consistent with the realities of the national and world scene and less and less misdirected by adherence to traditional stereotypes and clichés.

Perhaps the best summary of the social position of this movement is in the words of Dr. Harold Ockenga in 1960:

[The evangelical] intends that Christianity will be the mainspring in many of the reforms of the societal order. It is wrong to abdicate responsibility for society under the impetus of a theology which overemphasizes the eschatological.[18]

This new brand of evangelical recognizes the hypocrisy of telling people about love without offering them any tangible deeds of love to help meet their felt needs. It is reflected in three declarations of the statement unanimously adopted on April 16, 1966, by the Wheaton Congress on the Church's Worldwide Missions:

1) That we reaffirm unreservedly the primacy of preaching the gospel to every creature, and we will demonstrate anew God's concern for social justice and human welfare.

2) That evangelical social action will include, wherever possible, a verbal witness to Jesus Christ. . . .

3) That we urge all evangelicals to stand openly and firmly for racial equality, human freedom, and all forms of social justice throughout the world.[19]

The rising social consciousness of evangelicals is also reflected in the feeling of many that their churches

generally have sown the wind of a limited gospel and . . . now are reaping the whirlwind of a society structured very largely *apart from* the recognition of the gospel norms of Jesus' redemptive cosmic lordship and man's creation-wide mandate to obedient living as a servant of God. Not only man, but society itself needs the healing of the gospel principle. The gospel will dispense healing only when the harmonious biblical norms of love and righteousness are built into these societal structures. Jesus came to save the cosmos, including essential societal structurations. . . . Christ works through his people in bringing balm to festering societal structures.[20]

The Call to Recover Balance

Instead of seeking for churches that are *outstanding*, there now is an increasing effort to develop churches that are *out working* in the world. Those which merely stand like monuments to an outmoded tradition or museums of a glorious past are being forced to close their doors.

Statements about the need to combine evangelistic efforts with social involvement are increasingly common. Here are a few examples:

. . . the recognition of the social imperative of the gospel does not render any less important the matter of personal decision for Christ. It simply puts that decision in its proper context. It recognizes that a decision for Christ is at the same time a decision for the world, a decision for a renewed and reconciled humanity, a decision for the neighbor.[21]

It takes both the horizontal and the vertical to make the cross. The theology of horizontal social action without experiential vertical personal redemption is bankrupt. But, at the same time, an evangelism that preaches the vertical redemption of a life and does not produce horizontal social action is an irrelevant antique.[22]

We cannot substitute . . . evangelism for social concern. . . . If we do, we compartmentalize ourselves still further and bury God still deeper in the shrouds of irrelevance. We must rather unite these alienated partners in a holy and fruitful matrimony.[23]

The United States Congress on Evangelism in 1969 included a strong emphasis upon Christian social responsibility. Evangelist Leighton Ford of the Billy Graham Evangelistic Association was one of its clearest spokesmen. He challenged the church to match its profession with its acts, blending the concern for carrying out social implications of the gospel with concern for winning men to Christ. He maintained that men who have experienced Christ will act in their social concern as Jesus did when He walked on earth doing good. Sincere perfect love is not likely to prevail in present society, so Christians must give themselves in concern for justice. Above all:

A scheme to reconstruct society which ignores the redemption of the individual is unthinkable; but a doctrine to save sinning men with no aim to transform them into crusaders against social sin is equally unthinkable.[24]

At the same evangelistic conference numerous other speakers presented variations on Ford's theme. Dr. Myron S. Augsburger, for instance, called upon Christians to affirm the place of Christ's Lordship in judgment on social evils and aggressively permeate all strata of society with the gospel through a program for "evangelistic social action."[25] Senator Mark Hatfield appealed for removal of "the artificial polarization between those who preach the truth of individual conversion and the activists who proclaim some form of a 'social gospel,'" as well as of sharp distinctions between spiritual messages and social action, theological and social questions, and other false dichotomies.[26] Dr. Richard C. Halverson pointed out that

. . . when a congregation is spiritually healthy—that is, committed to Jesus Christ and to each other and constrained by a selfless concern for all men—evangelism will occur spontaneously, effortlessly, continuously, effectively. . . . Witness, by presence and performance as well as proclamation, is the product of the Spirit filled life.[27]

At Inter-Varsity's Urbana 70 Conference David Howard's keynote address referred to the similarity of the current crossroad to that of the student movement half a century earlier. The urge was to concentrate upon the racial, economic, and international issues of the day instead of upon evangelism, Bible study, and foreign missions.

One of the great mistakes made in 1920 and subsequent years was a polarization of issues. It became an "either-or" situation, either social concern or world evangelism. Today we dare not ignore the burning issues of race relations, economic injustice, and imperialism. By the same token we dare not ignore God's eternal and unchanging commands to His church to make the gospel of Jesus Christ, in all of its totality, available to all mankind.[28]

The Rev. Oswald Hoffmann, speaker on the "Lutheran Hour," indicated late in 1970 that the conflict in the churches between "social activists" and "personal salvationists" was fading in the mutual recognition that both are vital but that faith takes priority as a base for action. Those who made action primary are realizing that "without the inner content, it doesn't work"; faith is essential to produce loving action.

> Action is a by-product of faith, and to emphasize only the by-product without the product makes for a weak church. Without faith, nothing works, and the action is not really loving. People have sensed this.
>
> Indeed, there must be social action, but it has to grow out of what the apostles were sent out to proclaim in the first place. It has to have the ring of truth.[29]

Similarly, Dr. David Hubbard, president of Fuller Theological Seminary, has referred to the "growing middle ground" bringing together again the two conflicting strands of social activism and personal salvation which have torn modern church life into rival camps:

> The church has been wrongly polarized between these partial options. . . . But it is now being increasingly realized that social action can't be sustained without deep theological commitment and also that just preaching the gospel to reach individual hearts is not enough.
>
> Both the gospel and its social implications, both personal conversion and social action are involved in the mission of the church.[30]

Dr. Hubbard went on to indicate that drawing these elements together is producing a "new kind of activism" and a "great deal of spiritual excitement" through the active involvement of Christians in community affairs.

This parallels evangelist Billy Graham's message to the Central Committee of the World Council of Churches in 1967. He acknowledged that some evangelical Christians have de-emphasized the role of the church in social change, but he insisted that there is but one gospel, "the dynamic of God to change the individual and, through the individual, society"; we do not have a personal gospel and a social gospel. He emphasized that the great need today is conversion:

> If evangelicals have forgotten their social responsibility, it is due to a perversion in their teaching and a reaction against the "social gospel," but not because evangelism and the personal appropriation of Christ as Savior and Lord does not involve the individual in the suffering of humanity. . . .
>
> I have no doubt that if every Christian in the world would suddenly begin proclaiming the kerygma (gospel) . . . we would have a different world overnight.[31]

Critics may well say that such statements are "just talk." Talk plays an important role, however, in legitimizing the work of those who are actively trying to blend evangelism with social concern, and it stimulates the clergy and laity to change their conduct in the direction of their verbal behavior. With increasing pressures from youth and others to "put your money where your mouth is" and to make deeds coincide with creeds, the Great Reversal will soon be reversed. A few examples will demonstrate that the change is coming rapidly.

Examples of Evangelism Plus Social Concern

A decade ago there were only a few innovative efforts to reunite evangelism with social concern into a viable Christian witness, and they were widely scattered and largely unknown to people who were not directly involved in them. Recently, however, the situation has changed dramatically. The late 1960's saw the birth of numerous significant ventures, and the 1970's promise a sweeping revival of social ministries that combine the evangelistic and social-action thrusts.

Possibly the most popularized of these innovations are

related to the "Jesus People" movement, which spans a broad range of theological and practical orientations. Some are strongly Pentecostal; others are more clearly in the mainstream of evangelical faith. Their emphasis upon the importance of the new birth, diligence in sharing their faith with others, zealous service for Christ, joy in living for Him, and generous sharing of material resources, in many instances to the point of communal living, are among the distinguishing features of the movement that have captured popular attention and won a growing stream of followers.[32] Many view it as part of a genuine movement of the Holy Spirit similar to the primitive Christian church in Jerusalem, while others see it as a cheap but wholesome substitute for drug-induced experiences. At all levels they "are rethinking what it means to live what they believe, . . . reconstructing their lives so that professed priorities emerge as lived priorities."[33]

Spinning off from or closely related to the Jesus People movement are numerous other groups. One of the newest is the People's Christian Coalition, formed by evangelical seminarians, college students, professors, and artists, which publishes *The Post-American,* an "underground newspaper." Emphasizing that Christians must actively reject the values of corrupt society and radically resist its injustices, this group holds that both man and his social structures must be changed by Jesus Christ. Rebirth, new life, and justice point to fundamental changes in both man and society. "Radical Christians seek to recover the earliest doctrines of Christianity, its historical basis, its radical ethical spirit, and its revolutionary consciousness."[34] A grass-roots coalition to serve the Lord and serve the people, it focuses upon the ethic of Jesus Christ, which is both transcendental and comprehensive to all of life, and it dedicates itself "to active obedience to our

Lord and His kingdom, and to sacrificial service to the people for whom He died."[35] Not all "radicalism" is anti-Christian!

The Evangelical Committee for Urban Ministries in Boston (ECUMB) is an interdenominational, interracial association of evangelicals who are concerned about oppressed people in cities, the forces maintaining the conditions under which they live, and the general lack of positive and effective Christian response. Seeing the gospel of Christ as the good news of reconciliation between God and man which leads to a reconciliation between men, they are committed to advancing the total concern of the gospel with a balanced, holistic emphasis upon the spiritual condition and other needs. Its programs include tutoring, scholarships for black students in Christian colleges, volunteer service projects in several evangelical ministries in Boston, housing renovation, and the publication of *Inside,* a "forum for progressive evangelical thought" to inform Christians of the realities of urban life and their opportunities to become personally involved in meeting its needs.

Young Life has produced many leaders who have played a very significant part in melding evangelism with social concern. One of the outstanding examples is George Sheffer, who from 1961 to 1971 served in Chicago's inner city. There he combined demonstrating the love of Christ with verbally proclaiming it by helping powerless people meet their social, physical, psychological, and spiritual needs. Working with and through black people, he established food banks, clothing banks, and furniture banks. He stood by them when they were in trouble on the streets, at school, at police headquarters, and in the courtroom. He played the key role in the establishment of the Englewood Economic Development which unites whites with blacks in a business enterprise to reclaim industrial wastes and garbage, turning them into profitable resources and creating jobs. His testimony of the importance of the verbal testimony alongside good deeds is this:

From the very beginning of my work among angry, young, non-Christian Blacks, I've told them that I have a "Jesus Bag" and am sneaking up on them. If I did not tell them this was my reason for being there, later on they would call me a phony.[36]

Street worker Eddie Gist, himself a product of Young Life's efforts among the gangs of New York City, has commented on the polarization in the church between those who wish to keep Jesus in stained-glass windows, the pulpit, and little prayers and those who have observed hypocrisy and say churches should be burned down. He believes that Christians have the opportunity to be the third force between those polarized extremes if they will really follow Jesus Christ and not make "garbage" statements saying that the church should not get involved in social issues. Christians who instead stand up and tell the truth about society in the same way as Jesus did have the possibility of becoming that third force.[37] The "incarnational evangelism" of many Young Life workers is making a significant impact because it bridges verbal and nonverbal communication.[38]

The Salt Company, a Christian coffeehouse related to the First Presbyterian Church of Hollywood, California, has been fruitfully involved in innovative ministries since 1968. Not only do youth come to live musical performances in the coffeehouse, but teams also go to the ocean beaches to communicate Christ through free musical concerts and the spoken word. In the summer of 1971 five teams were working in various parts of the Los

Angeles area, five houses were used as crash pads and centers of witness in a loving community context, a drug rehabilitation ministry was helping many, the nonprofit Salt Company Mission From Hollywood, Inc., was providing arts and crafts work for youth, the Salt Company Art Company was operating "as a kind of Goodwill Industry" for the emotionally handicapped, and the church's board of deacons sponsored a broader job-seeking program known as "Operation Tentmaker." A contemporary free-flowing informal worship service aimed at new Christians and others whose needs were not satisfied by the more formal Presbyterian worship was held Sunday mornings and an evangelistic service Wednesday evening. A "continual stream of people" have come to know Christ as a result of these ministries.[39] Some of these have been described in pamphlets that can be purchased from the Salt Company.[40]

Since 1967 the evangelistic crusades of the Rev. Dr. Leighton Ford, an associate of Billy Graham, have included testimonies by committed Christians in social agencies. In addition to the usual invitation to the audience to commit themselves to Jesus Christ as Savior and Lord, an invitation has been given to help meet needs in local social agencies for volunteer services and finances. Ford sees this as fulfilling the obligation to witness to the whole of the biblical gospel and the concern of Christ for the lives of people. At the 1969 Congress of Evangelism in Minneapolis he gave a stirring address appealing to Christians to face the change and revolution confronting the world in partnership with Christ, the true revolutionary. In a subsequent book this theme is elaborated further, linking clearly the need for both personal evangelism and social concern in following the only course open to Christians in a world of revolutionary change: "to be

neither total resisters nor total rebels, but to be revolutionaries—Christian style!"[41]

The visit my wife and I made to The Church of the
Saviour in Washington, D. C., on January 31, 1971, was a
stirring experience. It coincided with a sermon by its
minister, Gordon Cosby, which was a summary of progress toward significant social reforms in numerous areas
of the city's welfare programs and political life that
resulted from the diligent and persistent but quiet work
of the mission groups of the congregation. A sense of
hearing a contemporary report of a new chapter of the
Acts of the Apostles overwhelmed me as I listened. This
experience was confirmed as I learned more and reflected
upon the significant achievements of that church's coffeehouse ministry, housing renovation, services to children, renewal of the neighborhood surrounding the Pot-
ter's House, meals and Bible classes for the elderly, and
plans for Dag Hammarskjöld College. The secret of their
success lies largely in the balance maintained between
the "inward journey" of engagement with self, God, and
others and the "outward journey" of engagements with
the world.[42]

Now I write with a similar sense of excitement, for like
the author of the Epistle to the Hebrews (11:32), time and
space fail to allow telling about countless other examples
of the effective wedding of evangelistic efforts with social
involvement that are sprinkled throughout our land. They
include the Crosscounter Program of Bill Iverson in
Newark, New Jersey; The Churchmen's Evangelical
Conference led by the Rev. Robert Henderson of Metair-
ie, Louisiana, which aims at ministering to the needs of
clergymen and lay leaders in order to establish and
maintain a wholesome balance between the tempting
polarities of contemporary life; the social service, relief,

and leadership programs of World Vision, all of which are under the umbrella of evangelism with an emphasis upon ministering to the whole man; the Evangelism-in-Depth ministries developed by the Latin America Mission in cooperation with other Christians, which are spreading to other nations and hemispheres and which often include social welfare ministries and witness to the social and political structures;[43] the inspiring story of the establishment of *Freedom Now* by the Rev. Fred A. Alexander to awaken white fundamentalists to their sinful racism and to stimulate corrective Christian action; its subsequent development into the highly significant magazine, *The Other Side,* which shares Christian perspectives, action, and information about the "forgotten Americans" who are hungry, defeated, miserable, discriminated against, and ignored; the University Church in Athens, Georgia, which combines a high level of social concern, emphasis upon the personal gospel, and open confrontation with intellectual problems related to Christianity in the context of a "high view" of the Christian Scriptures; the innovative ministries of the LaSalle Street Church and the Circle Church in Chicago and of the Calvary Presbyterian Church in the Hough area of Cleveland;[44] the ministries of special musical groups like the Exkursions which proclaim the gospel in out-of-the-ordinary places and thus attract people to Jesus Christ;[45] and the hundreds of neighborhood Bible study groups, prayer and discussion sessions, "house churches," coffeehouse ministries,[46] communitarian societies, underground churches, and other ventures both within and outside of religious institutions.

To list and classify the thousands of new programs and projects which have varying combinations of service, evangelism, societal reconstruction, fellowship, worship, and education would constitute a tremendous task; even within a single metropolitan area it would be difficult because most of them are so small, unpublicized, and disconnected from the normal church information channels. Many of them can be criticized for their narrow doctrinal perspectives, selfishly oriented focus of interest, anti-institutionalism (even while developing their own new institutionalized structures and action patterns), naive interpretations of social issues, and other defects, yet we should recognize that *there never has been an absolutely perfect Christian group.* Even Jesus' own inner circle of twelve disciples included one who betrayed Him, one who denied Him, a doubter, several who were greedy for status and power, and many who were weak in faith. God works through imperfect people and imperfect groups! (There are no others.)

In the midst of a significant proportion of these new movements is an emphasis upon both salvation and service that is much closer to the biblical ideal of a balance between evangelism and social concern than has characterized evangelicalism for two generations.

The new stance of evangelicalism is strongly two-legged in its ministry—one foot planted firmly in the gospel of personal trust in Christ as Savior and Lord and the other foot stepping out for right relationships with others, acting as responsible servants of Christ in the structures and issues of society.[47]

This new stance is clearly reversing the Great Reversal!

Problems in Evangelical Action

Nevertheless, the socially conscious evangelical tends to be frustrated. Seeing the broad scope of human needs, he hardly knows where to begin. He realizes that he could become so entirely caught up in social action or social welfare that he would have no time left for witnessing of the more conventional verbal kind, witnessing without which none can learn to know Jesus Christ as Savior. His evangelical brethren are slow to follow his lead except when his concerns can be used as "bait" for evangelism or touch upon problems of personal disorganization that they believe flow solely from the wickedness of the victims.

Difficulties may arise in relationships with other Christians, especially with fundamentalists who insist upon "complete separation from the world" and interpret it as demanding a refusal to cooperate with non-Christian groups for purposes of social action or social welfare. Such efforts to remain "pure" may actually result in even greater sin, as we have noted earlier, than is involved in cooperative involvements. They are inconsistent with the realities of the American political system in which coalitions of minorities often carry the balance of power. They ignore the fact that God often uses those who do not respect Him to fulfill His purposes.

Social, psychological, and material needs of people are so vast that it is very difficult for a church to decide which ones to try to meet. The good can become the enemy of the best. Avoiding duplication of effort can be one guideline, but it is important also to avoid the mistake of "churches that have spread themselves so thin in an effort to change society that they no longer have the resources to minister to the spiritual needs of individuals."[48]

A church so busily at work correcting the massive injustices of society that it cannot or will not make the effort to win men and women to an allegiance to Jesus Christ will soon become sterile and unable to produce after its kind.[49]

The wholesome balance between various types of ministries resides in the total congregation, not in individual members. "Others release me for my specialty by tending to their own."[50] This principle applies also to relationships between congregations, judicatories, and denominations. Some things are best done by the Christian as individual, some by the local church, and some by larger cooperative units on either denominational or interdenominational levels. The clarity of the precise Christian mandate to act is generally greater on the issues of evangelism and social welfare than of social action.[51]

It is easy to make the mistake of joining movements to combat social injustice too quickly and lightly. Christians have come to repent of many wars and the unrestrained nationalism that characterized their past; climbing carelessly on the bandwagon of current movements could lead to the need for similar repentance in the future.

What troubles me is that Christians conform to the trend of the moment without introducing into it anything specifically Christian. Their convictions are determined by their social milieu, not by faith in the revelation; they lack the uniqueness which ought to be the expression of that faith. Thus theologies become mechanical exercises that justify the positions adopted, and justify them on grounds that are absolutely not Christian.[52]

Frustration also develops as the socially alert Christian begins to see the wide scope of human needs with the compassion of his Lord, for despair results from his inability to deal with all of them. But he must recognize that Christians are not called to do so as individuals. They are all parts of the body of Christ; each has been given his own unique opportunities and gifts for the sake of the total body. Each can do something others cannot do, so all must support one another in the fulfillment of their differentiated portions of the total task.

In addition, no matter how active and consistent Christians are, new issues will continue to arise in our complex, rapidly changing world. Christians will do well to keep up with them and can never fully anticipate all of them, so problems of dealing rapidly and creatively with the new issues and then of keeping lines open for speedy communication of findings and recommendations will always be present. The better the channels of communication with innovators and scientists are, the easier it will be to keep abreast of change. The more solid the grounding of Christian commitment is and the better it is sustained by continuing Christian education, the more likely it is that the necessary responses will indeed be "Christ-like."

Frustrations also result from the feeling that Christian action is unnoticed, unheard, and unheeded. Faithfulness, however, will be respected in due time for its consistency, fidelity to Jesus Christ and the Scriptures, confrontation with the realities of modern society, efforts to see and share all pertinent evidence, and hence its tendency not to take adamant positions on dubious issues. When this materializes fully, the evangelical position will be true to the Christian faith that has been delivered once and for all. It will promote serving the whole man, for both personal redemption and social reconstruction will be goals. It will aid in the shunning of sinful worldliness, for it will reveal the immorality that is garbed in robes of light as well as that which appears in conventional evil forms. It will make evangelicals more kind and loving toward those who disagree with them, for they will recognize the complex, tenuous nature of problems and the web of contradictory values that cause sincere Christians to take opposing sides on many specific social issues. It will make them more obviously useful to a society that is beginning to recognize that its basic goals must come from outside of science. It will help men to be their brothers' keepers. It will lead them to put human values above property rights (people above things), so they will live in fact according to the principles that the body is more than raiment, a man's life does not consist of the relative abundance or lack of his possessions, and doing good to one of the least of Christ's brethren is doing good to Him.

Conclusion

Evangelicals for two generations have been primarily in the "comfort" camp which treats religious faith primarily as a source of personal gratification, compensation for real and imagined problems, and eternal salvation from sin and suffering. Meanwhile, Christians of more liberal theologies have tended to identify themselves with the "challenge" camp that emphasizes reforming the structures of society. Each orientation has tended to polarize itself, excluding values and actions supported by the other.

In regard to most social issues of this century, evangelicals are known for their negative positions—what they are against—rather than for a positive stand. They have worked for changed lives of individuals but not for changes in society, except as these might incidentally occur through converts. At the same time, they have described social conditions as going from bad to worse without recognizing that their own lack of social action to correct the structural evils of society and their professed "neutrality," which in reality constituted support of the power structure, were major factors contributing to the deterioration of social conditions.

As we have seen, however, evangelicals are awakening to their inconsistencies and returning to the totality of the Christian gospel. As a result, the old dichotomies between salvation and service, changing lives and changing society, proclamation and demonstration, man's vertical and horizontal relationships, personal piety and social service, faith and works, and believing and loving, all of which can be summed up in relationship to the contrast between evangelism and social concern, are breaking down. As Dr. Elton Trueblood stated recently, the great Christian word is AND—"the conjunctive genius." An either-or produces heresy.[53]

Awareness of the heretical nature of the Great Reversal that separated evangelistic zeal from social action is growing among evangelicals, and efforts to correct past mistakes are increasingly evident. As they allow the love of Christ to fill and transform them more completely, evangelical Christians again are beginning to move toward the forefront of social welfare and social reform in a truly biblical balance that views social action in a balanced perspective in relationship to evangelistic witnessing.

Socially conscious evangelicals realize that the avoidance of social involvement is equivalent to blessing the growth of evil in society. They confess their involvement in the sin of groups and institutions that cannot be attributed to any one or few persons. They acknowledge that neutrality is impossible with regard to social issues, for when they ignore these issues or "take no stand," they in effect give their blessing to the status quo or to whatever side is upheld by those who wield power in society. They are aware of the fact that maintaining aloofness from social issues is an act that proclaims an unintended message loudly and clearly to the world: "Our spiritual gospel is one of escapism; it has no relevance to the practical problems of life in the twentieth century." They heed admonitions of the New Testament to extend the love of Christ to all, not only to their Christian brethren. They know that truly loving men as individuals necessitates loving them in the aggregate as well. They accept the fact that Christians are often engulfed by social problems, and, instead of presenting conversion as the sole solution, they consciously include the social implications of the gospel in their Christian witness and service.[54]

Believing and loving are equally important in the Christian life (I John 3:18, 23-24), as are faith and works (James 2: 14-17) and the proclamation and demonstration of the gospel. Evangelism is both a product and a source of each. So also is social concern. Each is empty without the other. As evangelicals give attention intelligently, compassionately, and redemptively to both their evangelistic and their social responsibilities in the context of the total task of the Christian church, they have the opportunity again to become known for their enlightened leadership in society. Implementing the social implications of the gospel constitutes a return to fundamental truths of the Bible. It is producing a reversal of the Great Reversal.

Notes

[1]Arnulf M. Pins, *Contemporary Education for Social Work in the U.S.* (New York: Council on Social Work Education, 1966), p. 30.

[2]Walter Rauschenbusch, *Christianity and the Social Crisis* (New York: Macmillan, 1907), p. 346.

[3]Elton Trueblood, *The New Man for Our Time* (New York: Harper & Row, 1970). Compare Claude Thompson, "Social Reform: An Evangelical Imperative," *Christianity Today,* Vol. XV, No. 13 (March 26, 1971), pp. 588-592.

[4]Rev. Dr. David H. C. Read, as quoted in "The Unrest in U. S. Churches," *U. S. News and World Report,* Vol. LXII, No. 4 (January 23, 1967), p. 71.

[5]John Warwick Montgomery, "Evangelical Social Responsibility in

Theological Perspective," in Gary R. Collins, ed., *Our Society in Turmoil* (Carol Stream, Ill.: Creation House, 1970), p. 15.

[6]Howard Hageman, "Will Evangelicals Penetrate the Inner City?" *Eternity,* Vol. XXI, No. 1 (January 1970), pp. 23-25.

[7]Columbus Salley and Ronald Behm, *Your God Is Too White* (Downers Grove, Ill.: Inter-Varsity Press, 1970), p. 107.

[8]James G. Harris, "Evangelism and Christian Social Action—Is It Either Or?" (Fort Worth, Tex.: University Baptist Church, 1968; mimeographed).

[9]Don and John Ottenhoff, "Timothy Christian Schools," *The Other Side,* Vol. VII, No. 2 (March-April 1971), p. 25. For a vivid example of apathy, see Fred A. Alexander, "Operation Concern," *ibid.,* pp. 33-36, esp. p. 36.

[10]See Earl D. C. Brewer, "Social and Religious Indicators and Trends—Issues that Shape the Future," in Dept. of Long-Range Planning, *Workbook: Goals for Mission in the 70's* (New York: National Council of Churches, 1968), p. 41.

[11]For further Scripture references about the Christian's social responsibility, see David O. Moberg, *Inasmuch* (Grand Rapids, Mich.: Eerdmans, 1965), esp. pp. 31-58.

[12]See Bruce L. Shelley, *Evangelicalism in America* (Grand Rapids, Mich.: Eerdmans, 1967), pp. 21-24.

[13]Hans Mol, *Christianity in Chains: A Sociologist's Interpretation of the Churches' Dilemma in a Secular World* (Melbourne, Australia: Thomas Nelson Ltd., 1969), p. 17.

[14]Edward C. Lehman, Jr., "On Perceiving the Relevance of Traditional Religion to Contemporary Issues," *Review of Religious Research,* Vol. XIII, No. 1 (Fall 1971), pp. 34-41.

[15]Carl F. H. Henry, *The Uneasy Conscience of Modern Fundamentalism* (Grand Rapids, Mich.: Eerdmans, 1947).

[16]In addition to references given here, see "Suggestions for Further Reading" for examples. A summary also appears in Klaas Runia, "Evangelical Responsibility in a Secularized World," *Christianity Today,* Vol. XIV, No. 19 (June 19, 1970), pp. 851-854.

[17]For example, Arthur G. Gish, *The New Left and Christian Radicalism* (Grand Rapids, Mich.: Eerdmans, 1970).

[18]Quoted by Shelley, *op. cit.,* p. 113.

[19]Reported in M. R. DeHaan, "A Human Interest Story," *Freedom Now,* Vol. V, No. 1 (January-February 1969), p. 25.

[20]Paul Schrotenboer, "What Is!?" *Inside,* Vol. II, No. 3 (May 1971), pp. 26-27.

[21]Alvin C. Porteous, "Revival or Renewal: Recovering the Prophetic Dimension," *Foundations,* Vol. IX, No. 4 (October-December 1966), p. 329.

[22]The Rev. Wayne Dehoney, "Letter to Editor: Vertical and Horizontal," *Crusader,* Vol. XXIV, No. 7 (June 1969), p. 11.

[23]Arthur F. Holmes, "The 'Death of God' in the Evangelical Church," *Gordon Review,* Vol. X, No. 1 (Fall 1966), p. 12.

[24]Lawrence H. Janssen and Richard Hawley, "Congress on Evangelism Is Well-Attended Ecumenical Experience," *Crusader,* Vol. XXIV, No. 11 (November 1969), p. 6.

[25]Myron S. Augsburger, "The Making of Disciples in a Secular World," in George M. Wilson, ed., *Evangelism Now* (Minneapolis, Minn.: World Wide Publications, 1970), pp. 195-204.

[26]Mark O. Hatfield, "Evangelism and Coming World Peace," in *ibid.,* pp. 104-115.

[27]Richard C. Halverson, "Evangelism and the Renewal of the Church," in *ibid.,* pp. 91, 92.

[28]Robert Lehnhart, "Urbana 70," *Missionary Aviation,* Vol. XXVII, No. 2 (March-April 1971), p. 5.

[29]George W. Cornell, "Church Being Tested, Top Lutheran Says," *Milwaukee Journal,* December 19, 1970, Pt. 1, p. 5. See also Herbert P. Fritze, "Gospel Faith in Action Serves the Whole Man," *Lutheran Witness Reporter,* Vol. IV, No. 12 (June 16, 1968), p. 5.

[30]"Social Gospel, Theology Joined," *Milwaukee Sentinel,* May 29, 1971, Pt. 1, p. 21.

[31]"Graham Clarifies 'Social Gospel' Stand," *United Evangelical Action,* Vol. XXVI, No. 8 (October 1967), p. 25.

[32]See William S. Cannon, *The Jesus Revolution: New Inspiration for Evangelicals* (Nashville, Tenn.: Broadman Press, 1971), and Jon Reid Kennedy, "Dropping Out into Jesus," *Vanguard,* March 1971, pp. 7-9, 20-22. The most comprehensive survey of the movement is Ronald M. Enroth, Edward E. Ericson, Jr., and C. Breckinridge Peters, *The Jesus People: Old Time Religion in the Age of Aquarius* (Grand Rapids, Mich.: Eerdmans, 1972).

[33]G. Peter Schreck, *NLF Study on Biblical Model of Functional Church* (Boston: Evangelistic Association of New England, privately circulated Report No. 6, March 1971), p. 5.

[34]Jim Wallis, "Post-American Christianity," *The Post-American* (Box 132, Deerfield, Ill. 60015), Vol. I, No. 1 (Fall 1971), p. 3.

[35]"What Is the People's Christian Coalition?" *ibid.,* p. 5.

[36]Personal interview with George Sheffer, June 5, 1971.

[37]Eddie Gist, "I Know Who I Am," *Collegiate Challenge,* Vol. VIII, No. 1 (Spring 1969), pp. 21-22.

[38]See, e.g., the book about Bill Milliken, Young Life Leader on the Lower East Side of New York City: Bill Milliken and Char Meredith, *Tough Love* (Old Tappan, N. J.: Revell, 1968).

[39]Dr. Donald M. Williams, Minister to College Students, Hollywood Presbyterian Church, personal correspondence dated July 2, 1971.

[40]Evelyn V. Skinner, "Christ Still Works Miracles," n.d., and Donald M. Williams, ed., "Ten True Stories of Changed Lives," 1971 (The Salt Company, 1760 N. Gower, Hollywood, Calif. 90028).

[41]Leighton Ford, *One Way to Change the World* (New York: Harper & Row, 1970). See also "Social Action through Evangelism," *Christianity Today,* Vol. XI, No. 19 (June 23, 1967), p. 970.

[42]Elizabeth O'Connor, *Journey Inward, Journey Outward* (New York: Harper & Row, 1968), and *Call to Commitment* (New York: Harper & Row, 1963).

[43]W. Dayton Roberts, *Revolution in Evangelism* (Chicago: Moody Press, 1967), esp. pp. 83, 87-88, 97, 110, 114-117; "God's Love Must be Demonstrated," *Latin America Evangelist,* Vol. LI, No. 5 (September-October 1971), pp. 12-13.

[44]William E. Thomson, Jr. "Experiment in Biblical Christianity," *The Other Side,* Vol. V, No. 6 (November-December 1969), pp. 7-9.

[45]Dennis E. Shoemaker, "Joint, Rock and Christ," *Monthly Letter about Evangelism* (World Council of Churches, Division of World Mission and Evangelism), Vol. XIII, No. 3 (March 1971), pp. 1-3.

[46]John D. Perry, Jr., *The Coffee House Ministry* (Richmond, Va.: John Knox Press, 1966).

[47]Robert B. Munger, "God's Spirit Is Breaking Through," *Eternity,* Vol. XXII, No. 8 (August 1971), p. 14. For a parallel statement see Harold Z. Bomberger, "What the Church Is Doing Right," *Messenger* (Church of the Brethren), Vol. CXX, No. 10 (May 15, 1971), pp. 5-7.

[48]Bruce Larson and Ralph Osborne, *The Emerging Church* (Waco, Tex.: Word Books, 1970), p. 142.

[49]Ernest T. Campbell, *Christian Manifesto* (New York: Harper & Row, 1970), p. 9.

[50]*Ibid.,* p. 109.

[51]Jack O. Balswick, "Towards Consistent Christian Social Involvement," *Journal of the American Scientific Affiliation,* Vol. XXIII, No. 2 (June 1971), pp. 64-66.

[52]Jacques Ellul, *Violence: Reflections from a Christian Perspective* (New York: Seabury Press, 1969), p. 28.

[53]Elton Trueblood, "The Self and the Community," an address at the Conference on the Search for Reality sponsored by the Institute for Advanced Christian Studies, Des Plaines, Ill., October 1, 1971.

[54]For a brief summary of the scriptural basis for Christian social concern and practical means of fulfilling it see Moberg, *op. cit.*

Suggestions for Further Reading

Readers interested in learning more about the relationships between evangelism, social concern, and related
subjects are encouraged to read these books, which could
provide the nucleus for a library collection on the subject.

Campbell, Ernest T., *Christian Manifesto.* New York: Harper & Row,
  1970. The senior minister of the famous Riverside Church in New
  York City calls for a balance between personal and social applications
  of the Gospel, serving man's inner needs and the needs of society, and
  the horizontal and vertical dimensions of Christianity.
Clouse, Robert G., Linder, Robert D., and Pierard, Richard V., eds.,
  Protest and Politics: Christianity and Contemporary Affairs. Greenwood, S. C.: Attic Press, 1968. These essays by Christian historians
  and political scientists, including Senator Mark O. Hatfield, present
  Christian options on contemporary political issues in order to stimulate constructive social action.
Collins, Gary R., ed., *Our Society in Turmoil.* Carol Stream, Ill.:
  Creation House, 1970. Sixteen essays, chiefly by scientists who are
  members of the American Scientific Affiliation, deal with contemporary social problems and the Christian's response.
Ford, Leighton, *One Way to Change the World.* New York: Harper &
  Row, 1970. Stimulated by the 1969 U. S. Congress on Evangelism,
  this book by the vice-president of the Billy Graham Evangelistic
  Association passionately and intelligently describes "an evangelism
  that is both unquestionably rooted in the unchanging Gospel and
  realistically related to a changing world."
Gish, Arthur G., *The New Left and Christian Radicalism.* Grand Rapids,
  Mich.: Eerdmans, 1970. One of the founders of the Brethren Action
  Movement compares the New Left with the Anabaptist movement of
  the sixteenth century and presents the thesis that the Christian should
  be "radical," that is, go to the root of social issues by presenting a
  fundamental Christian alternative to the status quo.
Grounds, Vernon C., *Evangelicalism and Social Responsibility.* Scottdale, Pa.: Herald Press, Focal Pamphlet No. 16, 1969. The president

of Conservative Baptist Theological Seminary summarizes the biblical basis for Christian social ethics.

Hatfield, Mark O., *Conflict and Conscience.* Waco, Tex.: Word Books, 1971. A U. S. Senator shares his Christian faith and its contributions to personal and political life in this warm, thoughtful, and stimulating collection of speeches and essays.

Heasman, Kathleen, *Evangelicals in Action: An Appraisal of Their Social Work in the Victorian Era.* London: Geoffrey Bles, 1962. This excellent summary of the highly significant role played in British social welfare programs by nineteenth-century evangelicals supports Lord Shaftesbury's contention that "most of the great philanthropic movements of the century have sprung from the Evangelicals."

Hessel, Dieter T., *Reconciliation and Conflict: Church Controversy over Social Involvement.* Philadelphia: Westminster Press, 1969. The secretary for the Development of Social Analysis in the Board of Christian Education of the United Presbyterian Church presents the controversy, two models of social ministry, tensions between them, and his suggestions for an ethic of reconciliation.

Howard, Walden, *Nine Roads to Renewal.* Waco, Tex.: Word Books, 1967. The editor of *Faith at Work* presents nine authentic examples of church renewal which are related to small *koinonia* groups of deeply committed individuals.

Inside. Boston, Mass. 02118: Evangelical Committee for Urban Ministries, 387 Shawmut Ave. A bimonthly magazine which serves as "the voice of Christians living inside the city, directed towards those evangelicals desiring to understand and to erase the problems of racism and poverty."

Knight, Walker L., *Struggle for Integrity.* Waco, Tex.: Word Books, 1969. The tensions and experiences associated with significant changes toward community-centered and racially integrated programs in the Oakhurst Baptist Church, Decatur, Ga., are recounted by one of its members, a Southern Baptist executive.

Moberg, David O., *Inasmuch: Christian Social Responsibility in the Twentieth Century.* Grand Rapids, Mich.: Eerdmans, 1965. The scriptural basis and societal need for Christian social concern are summarized together with practical suggestions for its implementation and evaluation.

O'Connor, Elizabeth, *Call to Commitment.* New York: Harper & Row, 1963. The theological basis, founding, and missions of The Church of the Saviour in Washington, D. C., are described by one of its members.

O'Connor, Elizabeth, *Journey Inward, Journey Outward.* New York: Harper & Row, 1968. The balance between personal and social dimensions of the Christian life is presented in the context of further descriptions of the ministries of The Church of the Saviour, Washington, D. C.

The Other Side. Savannah, Ohio 44874: Fred A. Alexander, P. O. Box 158. A bimonthly magazine dealing with the role of evangelical Christianity in social action, this is the best source of descriptive and analytical articles written on the subject in popular style.

Pierard, Richard V., *The Unequal Yoke: Evangelical Christianity and Political Conservatism.* Philadelphia: J. B. Lippincott, 1970. A historian explains why evangelical Christianity must divorce itself from the idolatries of political, economic, and social conservatism.

Salley, Columbus, and Behm, Ronald, *Your God Is Too White.* Downers Grove, Ill.: Inter-Varsity Press, 1970. A white and a black evangelical relate Christianity to the oppression of blacks in American society and indicate positive responses to the objective and subjective needs of the black community.

Torney, George A., compiler, *Toward Creative Urban Strategy.* Waco, Tex.: Word Books, 1970. Fourteen essays which grew out of the 1968 Urban Church Seminar in Washington, D. C., present issues related to urban mission strategy.

Wirt, Sherwood Eliot, *The Social Conscience of the Evangelical.* New York: Harper & Row, 1968. The editor of Billy Graham's *Decision* magazine presents the thesis "that for a Christian to put his social conscience to work is to assert the true manhood that was destroyed by sin but restored in Jesus Christ."

Index

Act'vism, activists, 17, 18, 153, 165
Alexander, Fred A., 172, 180
Allen, Russell   , 66
Allport, Gordon W., 66
American Scientific Affiliation, 183
American Way of Life, 33, 42, 95 (*see also* Civil Religion)
Anderson, Clifford V., 10, 44
Anti-Semitism, 60, 62
Atheists, 53
Augsburger, Myron S., 163, 181

Babbie, Earl R., 52, 53, 64
Bachmann, E. Theodore, 118, 119
Balswick, Jack, 10, 182
Baptists, 55, 75, 117; American, 46, 49, 88; Southern, 18, 59, 108, 118
Baptists United for Spiritual Revival, 18
Barber, Mrs. Edward, 27
Barnes, Bill, 92, 103
Bear, Gordon, 10
Behm, Ronald, 180, 185
Benzel, Clifford, 10
Berelson, Bernard R., 84, 85
Berg, Norman W., 18, 89
Bethel College, 20

Bethel College and Seminary, 9
Bible, 25, 34, 35, 87, 120–126, 129, 145, 153–156
Biblical criticism, 36
Boice, James M., 148
Bomberger, Harold Z., 182
Bowditch, E. Francis, 26
Bowser, Lawrence C., 27
Bremmer, Robert H., 43
Brethren Action Movement, 183
Brewer, Earl D. C., 180
Brickman (cartoonist), 88, 102

Cairns, Earle E., 28, 43
Calvary Baptist Church, St. Paul, Minn., 17
Calvary Presbyterian Church of Cleveland, 172
Campbell, Ernest T., 9, 26, 182, 183
Campbell, Thomas C., 63, 66
Cannon, William S., 181
Catholics, 18, 54, 57, 75, 107, 108
Cayton, Horace R., 118, 119
Christ, 8 *see* Jesus Christ
Christendom, divisions in, 10, 13–15
Christian and Missionary Alliance, 31

Index

Church (es), 46, 124, 145, 159, 174–175, 184; crises in, 9–10, 15, 49; defection from, 95; mission or purpose of, 18, 52, 89, 154
Church of the Nazarene, 29–30
Church of the Saviour, 171, 184, 185
Churchill, Winston, 120
Churchmen's Evangelical Conference, 171
Circle Church, Chicago, 172
Civil Religion, 15
Clark, Henry, 103
Cleaver, Charles G., 103
Clergy, 48–52, 145–146, 166
Clouse, Robert G., 44, 183
Collins, Gary R., 44, 180, 183
Comfort, 52–53, 177
Concerned Presbyterians, Inc., 18
Conflict, 14, 47–52, 86 (see also Polarization)
Congregationalists, 55
Conservatism, 38–39, 42, 57–61, 94–98
Conversion, 21, 22, 38, 71, 80, 99, 113, 142, 147, 151, 154, 166; fractional, 127, 133, 148, 151 (see also Soul-winning)
Cook, Ronald J., 10
Cornell, George W., 181
Cosby, Gordon, 171
Coser, Lewis A., 102
Culver, Dwight W., 66
Curtis, Richard K., 44

Declaration of Independence, 139–140, 148

DeHaan, M. R., 180
Dehoney, Wayne, 180
Deprivation theory, 53, 63
Disciples of Christ, 18
Dittes, James E., 66
Dixon, A. C., 31, 32, 43
Douglass, H. Paul, Lectures, 53, 64, 65
Dynes, Russell R., 84

Ecological balance, 129–130
Ecumenical movement, 14, 71, 79, 83
Edgehill Methodist Church, Nashville, 92
Ellul, Jacques, 122, 147, 182
Englewood Economic Development, 168
Enroth, Ronald M., 181
Episcopal Church, 18, 31, 48, 49, 52
Episcopalians, 18, 55
Ericson, Edward E. Jr., 181
Ethicalism, 57–59
European Baptist Federation, 19
Evangelical(ism), 6–7, 14, 22, 25–26, 28, 35–38, 40–43, 46–66, 59, 62, 63, 87, 88, 94–95, 97, 116, 143, 150, 159–179
Evangelical Christian Education Foundation, 18
Evangelical Committee for Urban Ministries in Boston, 168, 184
Evangelism, 9, 13, 14, 15, 16–22, 25–26, 32, 48, 67–85, 86, 89, 99, 101, 104–119, 142–143, 144, 147, 150,

Index

Evangelism (*Continued*) 151–153, 154, 156, 157, 158–159; incarnational, 169; negative, 70
Evangelism-in-Depth, 172
Everett, William W. III, 10
Exkursions, 172
Extremism, political, 38–39, 93

Fahs, Ivan J., 10
Faith and Order Colloquium, 67
Faith and Works, 59, 94, 165, 179
Farley, James H., 102, 147
Fenton, Horace L., 10, 148
Finney, Charles G., 28, 89, 102
First Presbyterian Church of Hollywood, Calif., 169–170
Florence Crittenton Homes, 29
Foelber, E. E., 118
Ford, Leighton, 149, 163, 170, 182, 183
Forgiving, 54–55
Foster, Charles I., 43
Foster, Roland, 10
Foundation of Christian Theology, 18
Francis, Roy G., 10
Free will, 90
Freedom Now, 172
Fritze, Herbert P., 181
Fromer, Paul, 27
Frustrations in social action, 173–177
Fukuyama, Yoshio, 63, 66
Fundamentalism (-ists), 6, 7, 14–15, 21, 31, 34, 35, 37, 47, 50, 53, 70, 113, 117,

Fundamentalism (-ists) (*Con't*) 160, 172, 174; secularized, 39
Fundamentalist-modernist controversy, 14–15, 34, 37, 38–39, 104, 150

Gatewood, Willard B. Jr., 26
Gaudet, Hazel, 85
Gerth, H. H., 84
Gish, Arthur G., 148, 180, 183
Gist, Eddie, 169, 181
Glock, Charles Y., 52, 53, 57, 59, 62, 64, 65
God, 61, 129, 140, 173, 174
Gospel, 9, 29, 87, 111, 123, 150, 152, 154, 162, 165–166, 168, 177, 178, 179
Gouldner, Alvin W., 85
Graham, Billy, 15, 16, 27, 80, 102, 122, 134, 163, 165, 170, 183, 185
Great Commission, 155
Great Reversal, 9, 26, 28–45, 89, 101, 144, 150–182
Griffin, Clifford S., 43
Grounds, Vernon C., 148, 183
Grunstra, Bernard, 10
Guilt, 127–128, 143

Hadden, Jeffrey K., 48, 64, 91, 102
Hageman, Howard, 154, 180
Haines, Aubrey B., 94, 103
Hall, Clarence W., 27, 64
Hall, Edward T., 119
Halverson, Richard C., 164, 181
Hardberger, Phillip, 148
Hardin, Garrett, 148

Index

Harris, James G., 10, 180
Hartsock, Donald E., 44
Hatfield, Senator Mark O., 39, 44, 139, 148, 164, 181, 183, 184
Hawley, Richard, 181
Haymarket Riot, 33
Heasman, Kathleen, 43, 184
Hegy, Pierre, 10
Heinz, W. R., 65
Henderson, Robert, 171
Henriot, Peter J., 97, 103
Henry, Carl F. H., 35, 160, 180
Herberg, Will, 102
Heresy, 99, 109, 125, 178
Hessel, Dieter T., 184
Hill, Samuel S. Jr., 26
Hitler, Adolf, 125
Hitt, Russell T., 10
Hoffmann, Oswald, 164
Hofstadter, Richard, 39, 44, 103
Holmes, Arthur F., 181
Holmes, Urban T. III, 10, 43
Hostetler, John A., 85
Howard, David, 164
Howard, Walden, 184
Hubbard, David, 165
Hypocrisy, 13, 23, 25, 43, 56, 80, 91, 95, 100, 112, 138, 141, 157, 161, 169

Ideal types, 19–20, 22, 151
Idolatry, 89, 97, 121, 147, 185
Individualism, 30, 34, 36, 37, 89–92, 94, 98, 123–124, 161
Inside, 168, 184
Intentions, 129–131

Inter-Varsity Missionary Convention, 17, 164
Iverson, Bill, 171

Janssen, Lawrence H., 181
Jesus Christ, 8, 13, 20, 21, 33, 34, 36, 74, 99, 111, 113, 123–124, 126, 129, 135, 141, 144, 148, 154–156, 162, 163, 167–168, 169, 173; Second Coming of, 32, 37
Jesus People, 167
Jews, 23, 35, 54, 125
Johns, Sharron, 10
Johnson, Benton, 64
Jonah, 122
Jones, Jenkin Lloyd, 64
Jowett, John H., 28
Justice, 36, 113, 133, 163

Karrenberg, Friedrich, 147
Katz, Elihu, 84
Keith-Lucas, Alan, 118, 119
Kelly, George A., 118
Kennedy, 'Jon Reid, 181
Kerr, Willard A., 103
Kersten, Lawrence L., 59, 60, 65
King, Martin Luther, 55
Kingdom (of God, of Christ), 20, 21, 32, 35, 37, 40, 53, 76, 84, 107, 123, 152, 168
Knight, Walker L., 184
Krill, Donald F., 119

Landis, Paul H., 64
Larson, Bruce, 182
Larson, Donald N., 10

Index

LaSalle Street Church, Chicago, 10, 172
Latin America Mission, 172
Lazarsfeld, Paul F., 84, 85
Lehman, Edward C. Jr., 158, 180
Lehnhart, Robert, 181
Leming, Michael, 10
Leslie, William H., 10
Lewis, Gordon R., 10, 84
Liberalism, political, 39; theological, 6, 15, 18, 34, 47, 50, 57, 59–61, 62, 94–98, 117, 177
Linder, Robert D., 44, 183
Lindzey, Gardner, 118
Love, 36, 40, 98, 99, 100, 101, 109, 111, 113, 126–127, 131, 133, 135, 144, 155, 156, 157, 158, 161, 163, 165, 168, 178–179
Lutheran Men in America, 17
Lutheran Youth Encounter, 17
Lutherans, 55, 59–61, 62; American, 49; Evangelical Synod, 18; Lutheran Church in America, 111, 118; Lutheran Free Conference, 18, 19; Missouri Synod, 17–18, 49, 59, 108

Magnuson, Norris A., 43, 84, 85
Man, nature of, 74, 106–107, 115, 141, 145
Marty, Martin, 84
Marx, Karl, 53, 141
Marxian hypothesis, 53
Maxwell, Kenneth L., 26
McIntyre, Ruth, 10

McLarnan, Georgiana, 118
McLoughlin, William G. Jr., 44, 102
McPhee, William N., 84
Meehan, Brenda M., 43
Mehl, Roger, 102, 147
Meredith, Char, 181
Methodist Consultation on Evangelism in Latin America, 16
Methodists, 55, 75; United Methodists, 18, 49
Meyer, F. B., 28
Miller, S. M., 85
Milliken, Bill, 181
Mills, C. Wright, 84
Minorities, 38, 108, 132, 134, 137, 174
Missions, foreign, 109, 164; gospel (rescue), 38, 108, 109
Moberg, David O., 26, 44, 65, 84, 85, 102, 103, 119, 149, 180, 182, 184
Mol, Hans, 180
Montgomery, John Warwick, 8, 10, 36, 44, 179
Moody, Dwight L., 32
Morality, 23–24, 157
Motives, motivation, 105–119, 147, 152, 154, 156, 157, 159
Mott, Stephen Charles, 10, 149
Mueller, Elwin M., 10
Munger, Robert B., 182

National Council of the Churches of Christ in the U.S.A., 40, 48

Index

National Liberty Foundation, 10

Nazis, 23, 125

Neutrality, 87–89, 125, 142, 177, 178

Niebuhr, Reinhold, 27

Nishi, Setsuko Matsunaga, 118, 119

Oakhurst Baptist Church, Decatur, Ga., 184

Ockenga, Harold J., 44, 161

O'Connor, Elizabeth, 182, 184

Olsen, Marvin E., 103

Osborne, Ralph, 182

Other Side, The, 172, 185

Ottenhoff, Don, 180

Ottenhoff, John, 180

Pardee, Dennis, 147

Peale, Norman Vincent, 15

Pelham, Joseph A., 119

Pentecostal, 167

People's Christian Coalition, 167

Perry, John D. Jr., 182

Peters, C. Breckinridge, 181

Pierard, Richard V., 39, 44, 103, 183, 185

Pietism, 37, 63, 89, 90, 153

Pins, Arnulf M., 179

Pinson, William M. Jr., 10

Pluralism, 77, 78–79, 83, 110, 140, 146

Polarization, polarities, 6, 10, 17, 25, 34, 86, 94, 101, 164, 169, 171, 177–178

Politics, 50–51, 52, 88, 96, 115, 126–128, 139, 140

Porteous, Alvin C., 180

Post-American, The, 167

Poverty, 13, 29, 30, 32, 33, 34, 41, 42–43, 50, 88, 134–137, 172

Prejudice, 61–62

Presbyterian Lay Committee, 17

Presbyterian Layman, The, 17

Presbyterians, 55; United, 17, 48; U.S., 18; U.S.A., 49

Privatism, 91

Protest movements, 43, 132, 137–138

Protestantism, 89, 108

Protestants, 54, 57, 58, 59, 107, 108

Race, racism, 19, 78, 90, 123, 155, 162, 164, 172

Radical Christians, 161, 167–168, 183

Ramm, Bernard L., 44, 45

Ramsey, Paul, 103

Rauschenbusch, Walter, 24, 27, 179

Read, David H. C., 179

Redekop, Calvin, 97, 103

Regeneration, 24, 31, 152, 157, 160, 161 (*see also* Conversion)

Religious Bigotry Index, 62

Religious Research Assn., 53

Research, need for, 10–11, 37, 51, 53, 62, 67–85, 116–118, 157, 172–173

Resolutions, 40, 100, 136, 146

Revel, Jean-François, 141, 148

Review of Religious Research, 56

Revivalism, 20, 28, 90

Index

Revolution, 137–138, 139–143, 148, 170–171; Russian, 156

Reynolds, James F., 61, 65

Ringer, Benjamin B., 52, 53, 64

Riverside Church, N.Y.C., 9, 183

Roberts, W. Dayton, 182

Rokeach, Milton, 53–56, 57, 64, 65

Rokeach Value Survey, 54

Ross, J. M., 66

Runia, Klaas, 180

Sacraments, 70, 74–75

Salley, Columbus, 180, 185

Salomon, Elizabeth L., 119

Salt Company, 169, 170

Salvation, 29, 54–56, 57, 59, 73–75, 112, 152, 154

Salvation Army, 29

Scharlemann, Martin H., 118

Schreck, G. Peter, 181

Schrotenboer, Paul, 180

Schuman, Howard, 102

Scopes trial, 14

Secularization, 92, 102

Self-centeredness, 56, 136, 157

Selfishness, 126–127

Semantics, 72–73, 75

Shaftesbury, Lord, 184

Shaftesbury Project, 148

Shea, Terrence, 149

Sheffer, George, 168, 181

Shelley, Bruce L., 44, 180

Shibutani, Tamotsu, 118

Shoemaker, Dennis E., 182

Sin, 21, 99, 114, 128, 136, 142, 174, 178; social, 25, 120–149 (*see also* Social evil)

Skinner, Evelyn V., 181

Skinner, Tom, 46, 88

Slavery, 28, 124–125

Smith, Timothy L., 9, 30, 43, 44

Social action, 30, 33, 48, 86, 105, 142, 152, 158, 165, 166, 178

Social class, 78, 79, 95, 146 (*see also* Poverty)

Social concern (involvement), 9, 13, 14, 15, 16–20, 22–26, 35, 37, 42, 46–66, 84, 86–103, 104, 144, 150, 152–153, 155, 156, 158–159, 160–179 (*see also* Social action, Social Welfare)

Social Darwinism, 38, 92–94, 103

Social evil, 23, 28, 30, 34, 36, 101, 131–133, 137, 138, 144–145, 151, 153, 164, 177, 178 (*see also* Sin, social)

Social Gospel, 14, 15, 24, 31, 32, 33, 34, 36, 47, 150, 152, 160, 166

Social problems, 13, 19, 20–25, 42, 51, 87, 91, 98–99, 100–101, 105, 134, 144, 145

Social science, 48, 82, 83, 102, 157 (*see also* Research, need for; Sociology)

Social status, 50–51

Social welfare, 30, 38, 59–61, 104–119, 123, 142, 158–159 (*see also* Social work)

Social Welfare Index, 59

Index

Social work, 28–30, 104, 107, 109, 111, 113–114, 116, 150, 154 (*see also* Social welfare)

Sociology, sociological, 48, 59, 67–85

Soul-winning, 14, 20–22, 28, 32, 143, 144, 151 (*see also* Evangelism)

Spencer, Herbert, 103

Spencer, Sue W., 118

Spilka, Bernard, 61, 65, 66

Spurgeon, Charles H., 29

Stark, Rodney, 57, 59, 62, 65

State, church and, 115–116, 117–118, 125, 140

Stegman, Michael A., 102

Stipe, Claude E., 10

Stott, John R. W., 44

Strommen, Merton P., 65, 66

Suburbanization, 92

Summers, Gene F., 64

Sumner, William Graham, 103

Sunday, Billy, 33, 44

Talmadge, T. deWitt, 29

Tamminga, Louis, 88, 102

Tappan, Lewis, 43

Theologians, 40, 70

Theology, 6–8, 40, 49, 50, 51, 69, 72, 73–76, 161, 163, 175

Thompson, Claude, 179

Thomson, William E. Jr., 182

Torney, George A., 185

Toynbee, Arnold, 89

Traxler, Arthur E., 26

Trueblood, Elton, 148, 178, 179, 182

Twain, Mark, 120

U. S. Congress on Evangelism, 163, 170, 183

United Church of Christ, 18, 63

University Church, Athens, Ga., 172

Values, 54–56, 69, 91, 101, 132, 157

Vanecko, James J., 65

Voss, Robert, 10

Wagner, C. Peter, 64

Wallis, Jim, 181

Weber, Max, 73, 84

Wells, John, 10

Wheaton Congress on the Church's Worldwide Missions, 162

White, James B., 147

Willette, Diane, 10

Williams, Donald M., 181

Williams, Robin Jr., 65

Wilson, George M., 44, 181

Wirt, Sherwood Eliot, 185

Witness (ing), 72, 79, 101, 111–112, 115, 116, 164, 166, 173–174

Wolf, Hans Heinrich, 147

World Council of Churches, 19, 48, 165

World Vision, 172

Worship, 70, 112

Wyatt-Brown, Bertram, 43

Young Life, 168–169